ETHICS

Key Concepts in Philosophy

Key Concepts in Philosophy
Series Editors: John Mullarkey (University of Dundee)
and Caroline Williams (Queen Mary, University of London)

Mind: Key Concepts in Philosophy, Eric Matthews
Language: Key Concepts in Philosophy, José Medina
Epistemology: Key Concepts in Philosophy, Christopher Norris
Logic: Key Concepts in Philosophy, Laurence Goldstein

Ethics

Key Concepts in Philosophy

Dwight Furrow

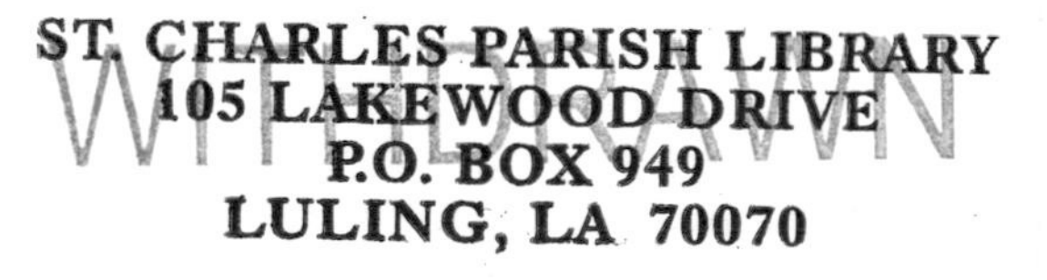

continuum
NEW YORK • LONDON

CONTINUUM
The Tower Building 15 East 26th Street
11 York Road New York
London SE1 7NX NY 10010

First published 2005

British Library Cataloguing-in-Publication Data
A catalogue record for this book is available from the British Library.

ISBN 0–8264–7244–3 (hardback)
0–8264–7245–1 (paperback)

Library of Congress Cataloguing-in-Publication Data
A catalog record for this book is available from the Library of Congress.

Typeset by RefineCatch Limited, Bungay, Suffolk
Printed and bound by Great Britain by
MPG Books Ltd, Bodmin, Cornwall

To Jordan
Who has taught me much about character

CONTENTS

INTRODUCTION

Moral philosophy is the systematic study of the nature of morality. Typically, when we study the nature of something, we learn new facts that we did not know before we began the study. We study biology because we want to discover new facts about natural organisms; we study economics because we want to understand the processes that explain how markets work. But morality is something most of us know about before we ever get to a college classroom. All societies have moral codes and most people by the time they reach adulthood know the rules or practices that make up that moral code. Most of us know that we should not kill innocent people, steal property that belongs to others, or become pathological liars, having learned appropriate conduct from various moral authorities in society. And most people by the time they become adults can give a passably coherent account of why morality is important – without it our social lives would be chaotic and difficult at best. Parents, teachers, religious authorities and community leaders are responsible for teaching morality. What can we learn through philosophical discussion that they have not already taught? Of course, some people apparently do not see the point of morality or were never taught morality in the first place, but I doubt that such people will listen to philosophers or authors if they are disinclined to listen to more familiar moral authorities.

To gain a sense of why it is important to subject morality to philosophical inquiry, we should view morality, not as collection of rules, but as a set of guidelines that we must apply to the very complex circumstances of our lives. We know that in general it is wrong to tell lies, but we also know there are circumstances when lying may be justified. Furthermore, our various moral considerations often come into conflict – we may have made incompatible promises, or be forced to lie in order to avoid breaking a promise. In order to make good decisions, it is not enough to simply know what rules we should follow. We have to know how to adapt those rules to our circumstances, and to do that effectively we must know why specific moral norms are justified. This is a philosophical question.

When we look just below the surface of morality – not just at the rules and norms but also at how we should apply them in specific circumstances – there is vast disagreement on moral questions. Most people know it is wrong to kill an innocent person. But is a foetus an innocent person? Reasonable people disagree on this question, so we need to find some way of thinking through an appropriate answer. In the contemporary world, given so much disagreement on moral questions, we must justify our beliefs and actions to others by giving coherent and intelligible reasons for our conduct. The philosophical task of clarification and justification can help us become better at articulating our moral point of view. Fuzzy thinking on these matters will get us into trouble, so all of us have reason to be reflective and thoughtful about moral questions.

Philosophy is one kind of reflection, though not the only kind. We can gain a good deal of insight just by living our lives consciously, thoughtfully, and with care, without ever opening a book of philosophy. However, this need to be reflective and thoughtful faces an obstacle. We do not always know much about the ideas we use in our moral reflections. We often learn to think and act in habitual patterns, the meaning and significance of which we do not recognize. The fact that we acquire our moral beliefs early in life is a good thing, because it allows us to grow up as social beings. However, it has a downside because we often take the moral concepts we have learned for granted and fail to see how factors in our social world can distort or corrupt our moral framework. Though our ethical concepts seem obvious and familiar to us, our limitations encourage us to misuse them. Some combination of weakness of the will, self-aggrandizement and sheer ignorance combine to conceal the deformation.

When our moral framework is seriously deformed, human misery is all too often the result. The episodes of mass death and misery in human history – religious wars, the slave trade, the Holocaust, to name just a few – were not moments in which ethical concerns were ignored. Each had their moral justifications that made them seem obvious and familiar to their perpetrators. The need to tell ourselves an ethical story about who we are is always present. But sometimes we can get that story tragically wrong.

Our social world is as much an ecology as our natural environment. When that ecology is out of balance, we often cannot see the problems without a wider perspective, one that takes into consideration the most basic elements of our human situation. We have to look beyond our everyday feelings and patterns of reasoning in order to find the hidden assumptions and meanings that structure our everyday lives without our knowing it. This is what moral philosophy helps us to accomplish. It is a form of self-understanding where what has been covered over by the sediments of our time can be unearthed and investigated. It is one of the ways we have of coming to know when we are getting our ethical story wrong.

It follows from this that one of the main tasks of moral philosophy is clarification. When reflecting about ethics in a systematic way, varieties of concepts naturally arise. If we are to begin to understand our moral situation, we must gain clarity regarding their meaning and function – hence the title and chapter headings of this book. Whatever the details of our moral story, it will emerge out of our understanding of the capacities that make a person a moral agent, the nature of moral reasoning, the goal of happiness, the nature of obligation, and the elements of character that make a person a good person.

How do we begin to clarify our moral concepts? One thing we might do is proceed as a scientist would, describing human behaviour and practices in the various contexts in which moral problems arise, explaining that behaviour by identifying motives, and developing theories about why people act as they do. We could do such an analysis of individuals, groups, societies or cultures and we could compare the results of that analysis in order to identify similarities and differences. The purpose of such an inquiry would be to describe and explain moral conduct, so we call this a descriptive inquiry. Historians, psychologists, sociologists, anthropologists and other social scientists are engaged in this sort of inquiry.

However, no matter how complete our description of moral conduct is, we can never discover through a descriptive inquiry what moral actions we ought to perform. It does not follow from the fact that we engage in certain moral practices that we *should* engage in them. Whether we should engage in them or not is an evaluative question, not descriptive. Philosophy is primarily concerned with the evaluative question. We want to know whether our moral practices are justified or not. Philosophy engages in a prescriptive, normative or evaluative inquiry in which we try to answer questions about what we should do.

The relationship between a descriptive inquiry about ethics and a prescriptive or normative inquiry is a subject of some dispute among philosophers. Most philosophers argue that 'ought implies can'. That is to say, what we ought to do must be related to what we can do. It is therefore important to link theories about what we should do to a conception of what we are capable of doing. As philosophers, we cannot proceed without an understanding of our moral capacities.

Our moral concepts and practices as we currently understand them provide an initially plausible account of our moral capacities. The everyday life of human beings must play an important role here. After all, our philosophical conclusions about what we should do must be tested. Ultimately, the test must be whether we can live in accordance with these conclusions and flourish. Since we have no way of experimentally testing philosophical viewpoints, the best we can do is compare them with our widely held common-sense beliefs to see if our philosophy exposes inconsistencies or inadequacies in common sense; or if common sense exposes the inadequacies of our philosophical theories. If we note inconsistencies between philosophy and common sense, we will have to make a decision whether to modify our philosophy or modify the common-sense belief. We ought to be reluctant to give up widely held beliefs if they play a practical role in our lives. On the other hand, common sense contains many irrational prejudices that it is the job of philosophy to expose, so we have to be prepared to give up those beliefs that upon analysis seem incoherent, dysfunctional or inconsistent with better supported beliefs. In attempting to explain our moral practices, philosophical reflection notes where those practices break down, and suggests reform. However, we still must make a decision about whether our vision of life with the reform is better than without it.

OBSTACLES TO MORAL PHILOSOPHY

There are many obstacles to getting moral philosophy off the ground. The belief that morality is wholly subjective and that any account of right and wrong is a matter of personal preference is one such obstacle. But a moment's reflection shows that it is virtually impossible to live by such a view of morality. Suppose that your mother is raped. The judgement that something deeply important has been violated is not an optional belief that one could have or not have depending on one's current preferences. To love someone is, in part, to care about her welfare. To fail to see such an action as wrong is to fail to have the appropriate attitudes that constitute love. Given that one's survival matters and that we must depend on others for survival, the welfare of other people as well as our own welfare cannot be a matter of indifference. That I like chocolate is a matter of personal opinion, but only because my liking chocolate has no moral consequences. If my enjoyment of chocolate were somehow to induce psychotic reactions among my friends, it would no longer be a matter of indifference. All of our relationships depend on our ability to make defensible evaluations of conduct. Only someone who cared about nothing could view moral judgements as purely a personal preference. Happily, such people are a minority.

Another obstacle to moral philosophy is an excessive reliance on religion as the source of morality. If it is the case that in order to thoroughly understand morality, all we need to do is consult religious authorities, then moral philosophy has no point. There would be no reason to think through moral questions philosophically, since the answer to these questions is more readily available elsewhere.

Religion and morality are related because religion has been, throughout much of human history, the primary vehicle through which cultures transmit moral beliefs. However, empirically, the connection between religion and ethics does not appear to be particularly strong, since there are good people who lack a religious commitment and some very bad people who are believers. Furthermore, appeals to a religious perspective do not settle moral questions. This is, in part, because foundational texts that contain moral teachings must be interpreted by human beings and must use human standards of assessment. Furthermore, there are a variety of religions with a variety of moral practices. Without some independent way of assessing the various religions, there is no way of determining which one is correct.

However, there is a deeper reason why religion cannot be the ultimate authority on moral questions. Monotheistic religions claim that God commands what is right and wrong. According to divine command theories, what makes an action right is that God commanded us to perform that act. On this view, God is the ultimate source of all morality. But by what standards does God judge an act right or wrong? There can be only two possible answers to this question. Either God judges an act right or wrong based on reason. Or, God uses no criteria at all and judges arbitrarily. If God issued his commands arbitrarily then there are no standards to which the judgement conforms and it could have been the case that murder, rape and torture were commanded by God. Apparently, this is not what God did, but God could have done so since God is omnipotent.

However, this has unwelcome implications. Morality is, on this view, arbitrary, a product of God's whim since reason was not involved. Had God commanded rape, murder and torture then divine command theory implies that rape, murder and torture would be praiseworthy, and we would have no rational grounds to object since morality is not based on reason. Intuitively, it seems that such acts could never be praiseworthy and false that we could have no valid argument against such a possibility. If we are to take morality seriously, it cannot be whimsical or arbitrary. Moreover, if God judges arbitrarily, God could not be the supremely rational being she or he is alleged to be. A supremely rational being could not choose something arbitrarily. Therefore, this option seems wholly unacceptable.

Suppose, then, that God commands what is right and wrong based on reason. If so, the content of the reasons make an action right, not the fact that God commanded it. Thus, morality is a standard independent of God to which God appeals, and we must engage in philosophical reasoning to understand it. Since the first option entails an unacceptable account of morality, we are forced to conclude that divine command theory is false.

This is not to deny that religion may play an important role in providing people with an understandable, moral framework they can rely on and models of admirable conduct to emulate. However, it cannot take the place of rational reflection on moral questions.

Once we have these misunderstandings out of the way, we can proceed to think about the nature of morality with the hope of finding those elements in our moral lives that make sense and how they hang together in a comprehensive vision of moral life. The aim of this book is to introduce the main elements of the moral conception that characterizes Western society. Some of these elements have roots in our intellectual history. We cannot understand our contemporary moral views without understanding some of these historical roots. Thus, part of this investigation will highlight themes in the history of moral philosophy. However, as anyone who has picked up a newspaper recently knows, our moral lives undergo continual change, and so does moral philosophy. Thus, we will pay close attention to a variety of trends in contemporary moral philosophy as well.

In addition to providing a survey of the field of moral philosophy, this text will develop a point of view. Philosophy is emphatically not about accepting doctrine from authorities but involves critically engaging beliefs to see if they withstand scrutiny. Although it is important to learn about what other philosophers have said on a given topic, we can understand philosophy only by practising it. Therefore, I try to convey some of the excitement of doing philosophy by developing arguments and treating objections. These positions are likely to be controversial, but this is as it should be. Controversy is inherent in the practice of philosophy.

Given the aim of developing an extended argument, the broad outlines of my argument are as follows. As we have seen, moral philosophy enables us to evaluate whether the story we tell ourselves about our moral context is reasonable or not. The principle theories of ethics that dominate our moral tradition – utilitarianism and deontology – once did precisely that. (I will describe these theories in detail in the chapters that follow). These theories are products of the eighteenth century, a century devoted to overturning the privilege of rank that had characterized the monarchies of Europe until that time. These theories exposed the injustice of inequality by emphasizing the importance of impartiality and objectivity.

Today we face a different challenge. Those eighteenth-century theories located moral authority in an abstract ideal of rational perfection. As a consequence, philosophical ethics has seemed impractical, unattainable and incompatible with the satisfactions of life. Furthermore, these theories obscure the real source of moral authority – our relationships with others on whom our flourishing depends. This misunderstanding regarding the source of moral authority has allowed a corrosive form of individualism to survive, which can be overcome only by taking our relationships seriously, or so I shall argue.

CHAPTER 1

MORAL AGENCY

If we are to come to some conclusions about how we should live and what specific obligations we have toward others, we need to begin with an understanding of human nature and what makes human beings tick. It would be useless to come up with a conception of morality that human beings could not live by or could adopt only with great difficulty by sacrificing some other essential component of human existence. Thus, we want to begin our inquiry by discovering what motives are in play when people act morally and provide an account of what makes moral conduct intelligible to us. In other words, we want to know what enables human beings to be moral agents.

An agent is someone who acts; a moral agent, then, is someone who has the ability to make moral decisions, and to act on them. What are the capacities that enable us to make moral judgements? Most philosophers today would agree that, at the very least, in order to be moral agents, we must have the capacity to make our own decisions and act on them. This is because we hold moral agents responsible for their actions and praise or blame them depending on how we evaluate their actions. If we do not make our own decisions, if our actions are not under our control, the practice of praising and blaming people for them would make little sense. Thus, a basic requirement for moral agency is autonomy. I will refine this definition shortly but, for now, we can define autonomy as the ability to make one's own decisions, to be a self-directed person.

It follows that children and non-human animals, not to mention inanimate objects, are not moral agents. Of course, children gradually acquire autonomy and therefore moral agency as they gain control over their actions. And animal psychologists have uncovered some evidence of moral behaviour in other primates. However, it is doubtful that animals have the level of control needed to qualify as full moral agents, as far as we know.

A moral agent not only acts autonomously; she must be capable of moral actions as well. What kinds of actions count as moral actions? This is a topic of some dispute, and how one answers this question depends on which theory of morality one endorses. Rather than get into those disputes now I will stipulate that moral actions are those that most people take to be paradigm examples of moral actions. When we tell the truth, keep promises and assist others in need or avoid harming them we are engaged in moral conduct.

These are commonplace examples of moral conduct, but some moral actions are extraordinary and heroic. When people save lives at some cost or risk to themselves, their actions fall under the general category of moral actions as well. Heroic actions are interesting because of what they reveal about our moral capacities. So I want to begin our analysis of moral agency by focusing briefly on heroic moral actions.

The example I prefer is that of Oskar Schindler, the rescuer of Jews during the Holocaust, and subject of the film *Schindler's List*. I prefer Schindler because he is, like most of us, complicated. Oskar Schindler was, at least in some respects, a heroic figure, though not a saint. Schindler was a successful German industrialist operating in Poland during the Nazi occupation. His main business was to manufacture various items for the German war machine, while chasing every attractive skirt in Crakow. His wife, aware of his infidelities, remained at home in Germany. Schindler maintained cordial and co-operative relationships with the Nazis and was, at first, tolerant of their repressive policies towards Jews. However, when Schindler's Jewish office manager was taken to the train depot to be shipped to what was euphemistically referred to as a 'labour camp', Schindler went to some lengths to personally retrieve him and was confronted with the inhumanity of shipping massive numbers of human beings in railroad cars designed for cattle. Schindler's further investigations lead him to discover the brutality of the Nazi regime, and at considerable risk to himself and his business, he was to undertake elaborate schemes to protect his workers and sabotage the German war machine.

Why would someone like Schindler take such a risk in order to benefit others? Are there any similarities between Schindler's actions and more ordinary moral acts? Most of us will never save the lives of hundreds of people. Yet, the experience of feeling obligated to do something for others even when it might go against our interests is a common human experience. Most of us, at least some of the time, help others when our help is needed, tell the truth, keep promises, respect the property of others, etc., even when these actions will cost us something. Why? If moral actions are actions that we choose, why do we choose to engage in actions that benefit others but not ourselves?

SELF-INTEREST

Typically, we act because we want to achieve a purpose or satisfy an interest or desire. We go to work to earn money, cook dinner to satisfy hunger, etc. So perhaps we can answer our questions about the motivation for morality by identifying the purpose or desire that it serves. Is there some purpose or interest shared by most human beings that would explain our moral conduct? What purpose or interest was Schindler's actions serving?

Human beings are diverse, each of us unique in a variety of ways, so there may not be a single thing that all of us want. However, we may all be driven by a common motive – self-interest. Think about the variety of actions that you perform each day. Don't you perform them because you are trying to advance your interests?

Some thinkers have argued that self-interested motives explain all our actions. Thus, any plausible account of morality would have to show how morality helps us get something we want. We call this account of human motivation psychological egoism. Psychological egoists argue that human beings always seek to maximize their self-interest.

In addition to being self-interested, human beings are rational as well. We are able to find effective ways of satisfying our self-interest. If I am a rational egoist, I know that it is human nature to always look out for myself. I also realize that other people are also looking out for themselves and will not only prevent me from getting what I want but will try to take what I have. So in order to get some of what I want, I compromise. I agree to give up some of my desires and follow moral and legal rules as long as other people are willing to do the same. I am still acting out of self-interest but, most of the time, it is in my interest to co-operate with and help others. Nevertheless, when our individual interests conflict with the interests of others, and we can get away with it, we will invariably choose to act on our own interests, according to the psychological egoist. The institutions of morality thus arise from purely self-interested motives. Some psychological egoists have thought of morality as a social contract in which I give up some of my freedom in order to gain security.

Psychological egoism generalizes about all human action, and that leaves the theory open to some obvious counter-examples. Most of us have helped an elderly neighbour go shopping, told the truth when we could get away with a lie, donated food at Christmas time, or perhaps, like Schindler, saved lives. But according to the psychological egoist, though we may not be aware of our true motives, they are nevertheless selfish. Morally good actions make us feel good, offer the possibility of reciprocation in the future, make us look good in the eyes of others, or enhance our chances for salvation, and we perform them for those reasons. Apparently, the psychological egoist can explain away any counter-example.

Psychological egoism is attractive to many people because it seems hardheaded and realistic in its understanding of human nature or because it reinforces the suspicion that there are deep layers of hidden meanings in human experience that most of us are unwilling to recognize. However, when we unpack the position its plausibility disappears. Schindler's actions seem to be a counter-example. We don't know enough about Schindler to be very accurate in assigning motives to him – what we know about him suggests that he was far from being a person with exemplary character. We can imagine that he received a variety of satisfactions from rescuing his Jewish workers – perhaps he enjoyed the thrill of deceiving the Nazis or perhaps the feeling of people being dependent on him enhanced his self-respect. Let's assume that Schindler's actions did enhance his self-respect and that he took pleasure in the thrill of his deceptions. And let's assume that these satisfactions were part of his motives for continuing the dangerous mission. It does not follow from this that he did not also genuinely care for the welfare of his workers. The fact that we receive satisfaction from an action does not entail that the pursuit of that satisfaction is the primary motive. I get satisfaction out of successfully playing a difficult passage on the guitar. But the goal of my action, and the object of my desire, is to reach the end of the passage successfully – I am not aiming at the satisfaction. The satisfaction is a by-product of the action.

The point here is that human beings are complex with a variety of desires, each with their own distinct object, and our actions are often explained by many desires operating simultaneously. Yet, the psychological egoist must assert that all of our desires have only one object – our own self-interest.

To see why this is implausible imagine two hypothetical Schindlers – Schindler 1 and Schindler 2. Schindler 1, after the war, receives an unexpected guest at his home who informs him that a band of surviving Nazis systematically hunted down and killed all of the people he rescued. Schindler 1 receives this news with indifference and invites the bearer of this news to share a beer to celebrate the victory of a local sports team. By contrast, Schindler 2, after receiving the same guest, is inconsolable for days, psychologically shattered by the horrible news, and inquires if there is anything he can do for the surviving family members. Surely, our imaginary Schindlers, in rescuing their workers, would not have been motivated by the same desire. Furthermore, the best explanation of Schindler 2's response is that he genuinely desired to advance the good of others independently of his self-interest. At this point, he has nothing to lose by the demise of those he rescued, but his feelings indicate a genuine concern for their welfare nevertheless. I think most of us know people who would have responded to a similar situation as Schindler 2 did. In fact, I suspect Schindler 2's response would be the more common response. The best explanation of this common response is that human beings are, at least some of the time, motivated by a genuine concern for others, usually expressed as empathy, sympathy or compassion.

Of course, the psychological egoist can always argue that our actions to benefit others satisfy some deep, unconscious, psychological need. However, if that is the case, the only way to satisfy that need is to have as one of our goals the good of others.

This argument shows that psychological egoism cannot explain all human action. At least some human beings are psychologically capable of what I will call economy-size altruism – acting, at least in part, out of genuine concern for the wellbeing of others. Moreover, Schindler appears to be capable of an even more extensive form of altruism. He is capable of sacrificing his most important interests for the wellbeing of others – super-size altruism.

In fact, most human beings have some capacity for super-size altruism, although perhaps not to Schindler's degree. Suppose that you are running late to a job interview that promises to secure a significant career advance and a substantial raise. It is January in Boston, cold, with snow beginning to fall. Cutting through an alley to save time, you stop dead in your tracks when you hear a baby's cry coming from behind a row of garbage cans. You discover that a baby has been abandoned, wrapped only in a thin blanket. There is no one nearby, your cell phone battery is dead, and if you stop to help you will surely miss the interview and sacrifice your chance to land the new job. Nevertheless, most people would stop to help. Why, if we are incapable of putting the interests of others ahead of our own? In fact, soldiers, doctors and nurses who deliver aid in emergencies, firefighters and police sometimes sacrifice their lives for strangers. Super-size altruism though far from ordinary is a significant feature of our moral lives.

However, it may be that, although we are capable of altruism, we are fools if we allow altruistic feelings to motivate us. Perhaps the rational thing to do is to always act to advance our self-interest. This position is called ethical egoism. The ethical egoist says that we should always do what is in our self-interest and we never have an obligation to advance the interests of others. Ethical egoism avoids the problems that psychological egoism had in accurately describing our motives. The ethical egoist is not describing our motives but is advocating an approach to making decisions.

This view seems compelling to many people because, once again, it appears to advocate hard-headed, unsentimental rationality while pointing us towards the worthy pursuit of personal happiness. Furthermore, it is important to acknowledge that an ethical egoist will not necessarily be a moral monster. Like the rational psychological egoist, a rational ethical egoist would recognize it is in her long-term self-interest, most of the time, to be co-operative, helpful, and to follow moral norms. However, when co-operation is not to her advantage, she should look to her own interest only.

Again, despite the superficial attractions of this view, its plausibility disappears under scrutiny. First, a world in which everyone was an ethical egoist would be a world in which people would refrain from co-operating or following moral norms unless there were clear self-interested reasons to do so. It is reasonable to conclude that people who are reluctant to co-operate or hesitant to follow moral norms would be less trustworthy and slow to resolve disagreements allowing conflicts to be even more persistent than they are in today's contentious world. It is hard to see how a world of greater conflict would be to anyone's advantage.

Furthermore, how could someone consistently advocate ethical egoism? To do so would be to advocate that others also act in accordance with their own interests, which will often conflict with yours. Thus, if they take your advice seriously you would be advocating against your interests, which would violate the basic principle of egoism. Therefore, to avoid violating her own principle, an egoist must advocate egoism for herself and for anyone else who shares her interests in a particular situation but advocate altruism for others. Such a level of dishonesty and incoherence would be hard to sustain, especially in contexts where trust and consistent patterns of judgement are necessary to accomplish practical tasks. Imagine an ethical egoist trying to teach a child when to tell the truth. Dad says 'always tell the truth to me, but only sometimes to your mum, when your honesty won't hurt me.' Of course, Mum, an ethical egoist as well, is giving little Johnny the very same advice. What exactly is little Johnny to do?

These inconsistencies aside, there are deeper and more informative difficulties with ethical egoism. Social scientists often make use of a device called the prisoner's dilemma to point out the difficulties with a society of rational egoists. Suppose the FBI arrests Heather and Gordon for hacking into a bank's computer system, though the evidence is not as strong as the prosecutors would like. Heather and Gordon are brought to the federal building for interrogation and put in separate rooms, and the FBI offers each of them the same deal. The following conversation ensues between the FBI and Heather.

> Heather, if both of you refuse to confess, we will have to admit that we lack enough evidence to convict you of hacking, but we will jail both of you for one year for possession of illegal software. But, if you turn government's witness and help us convict Gordon, then you will go free, and Gordon gets twenty years in prison. However, if you don't confess and Gordon does, then he will go free and you will get twenty years. So what is it going to be?

Heather thinks for a minute and then asks, 'Suppose both of us confess?' 'If you both confess you both get ten years,' responded the agent.

So Heather thinks,

> Suppose Gordon confesses. If I don't confess I will get twenty years. But if I do confess, I'll only get ten years. On the other hand,

suppose Gordon doesn't confess? If I don't confess either, I'll go to jail for a year. But if I confess and he doesn't, I'll go free. So it doesn't matter what Gordon does. I should confess.

Remember that Gordon, being rational, is using the very same reasoning. Thus, both of them confess and both go to jail for ten years. The FBI, of course, are very happy, because if both had remained silent, they would have gotten only a year in prison. Notice that if Gordon and Heather had co-operated with each other and not confessed, they would have been better off. The problem of course is that if Heather decided, in the interests of co-operation, that she should trust her partner, Gordon might have taken advantage of her, and then her goose would have been cooked. Thus, it will always seem to be an advantage to not co-operate. This leads to what social scientists call the free-rider problem. The best-case scenario for the egoist is that everyone else co-operates, except for her, so she can reap the benefits of their co-operation while incurring none of the costs. But, in this case, Gordon was savvy enough not to be a sucker. The moral of the story is that being self-interested does not always get us what we want. If Heather and Gordon had trusted each other rather than pursuing their self-interest, they both would have been better off. The ethical egoist is offering us some bad advice.

The difficulty with ethical egoism is that it does not take seriously the many situations in which co-operation is necessary and the kinds of motivations that make people reliable co-operators. If you are the sort of person who always acts self-interestedly, what will other people think of you? What kind of long-term reputation will you have? If people find out you are the sort of person who will be reluctant to co-operate they may be less willing to enter into agreements with you that might be to your advantage. Thus, it is to your advantage to co-operate even it might cost you in the short term. In fact, it will be to your advantage to develop the habit of keeping promises, telling the truth and being helpful and considerate because this will help insure that, in the future, others will treat you in a similar fashion.

Notice, however, that this reasoning falls well short of requiring altruistic motives. A rational egoist might grant that we should usually appear to be an honest, reliable co-operator because it is to our advantage when others see us in that way. But, when we can get away with being dishonest or selfish without harming our reputation we should look to our self-interest. Again, the ethical egoist is giving us bad advice. The problem with this as an approach to life is that we cannot count on successfully hiding our real motives from people. If we only pretend to be concerned about others, our pretence is likely to be exposed. We reveal ourselves to others in countless ways that give them clues to the attitudes and desires behind our actions. When we reveal selfish motives, we have to deal with the consequences of mistrust, which can undermine any pursuit that requires co-operation.

Furthermore, ethical egoism cannot explain our capacity for ordinary social interaction. The need for the egoist to disguise her motives will inhibit the development of effective patterns of behaviour. Think about the degree to which your daily activity is habitual and routine. Most of the time, our actions and interactions with others are not the product of conscious, deliberate planning. We don't carefully construct each sentence in conversation or thoroughly calculate the costs and benefits of each option available to us when making ordinary decisions. Most of our actions flow effortlessly from a kind of default responsiveness to reality that reflects patterns of thought and feeling we have built up from many years of experience. This is a good thing because otherwise we would not be able to drive while carrying on a conversation or interact with a group of people where we have to process a variety of information streams simultaneously. In social contexts, if we could not rely on our habits of thought and feeling, our dealings with others would be laboured and clumsy, like a centipede that must think how to move each leg in order to walk.

Similarly, responding to situations in morally appropriate ways requires habits of thought and feeling – motives – that shape our actions in ways that make them effective. Honesty that succeeds in giving people confidence in you requires a genuine concern for the truth. Only a person who is practised at weighing the genuine importance of the truth in a variety of circumstances can be honest without tactlessly harming others, thereby making people suspicious of her motives. Helpfulness of the sort that people actually welcome because it is beneficial, requires a genuine concern for the person who needs help. Otherwise, we risk interfering in the lives of others in ways they would not welcome, thus making others reluctant to seek our co-operation.

The point here is that faked motives – which disguise self-interest – seldom produce effective action because the patterns of feeling and thought required to make our actions effective are lacking. To put the point succinctly, if you ask someone for help and she has to think too much before responding, look for assistance elsewhere.

Yet, the ethical egoist is advocating that we be like the aforementioned centipede. According to the egoist, in situations where selfishness would cause mistrust, we should rely on the motive of self-interest, calculating where our advantage lies, but disguise it by acting as if one is not self-interested. Only the most skilled con artist can reliably pull this off. For most of us, in many situations our actions must flow from our real motives if they are to be successful, which at least some of the time must include a genuine regard for the interests of others.

Finally, ethical egoism is even less plausible when we consider close relationships – friendships, romantic and family relationships, workplace collaborations, etc. For example, suppose you have a successful and highly satisfying career. Your spouse, who is unhappy in her job, gets a job offer that will dramatically increase her career satisfaction, at an income equivalent to yours. Unfortunately, your spouse's new job will require a move across country requiring that you give up your current job, with uncertain prospects for reviving your career at the new location.

The egoist advocates that you should pretend to consider your spouse's interests but resist any decision to make the move since to do so would be against your interests. Only if your spouse threatens to leave you and you value your relationship more than your job should you genuinely consider moving. If your spouse is an egoist as well, such threats seem inevitable. However, a relationship in which threats and counter threats are required to get the partners to genuinely consider each other's interests is unlikely to be happy or successful. Of course, there is no correct answer to what our hypothetical couple should do. They will have to work this out for themselves. But whatever the decision, the outcome is likely to be one they can live with only if both partners take the interests of the other into account. The problem with ethical egoism in intimate relationships is that, if we consider the interests of others only when threats raise the stakes so high that being inconsiderate threatens one's own interests, ordinary decisions become tumultuous scenes of conflict and risk-taking in which accommodation occurs only after much damage to the relationship has already occurred.

The conclusion to draw here is that we have self-interested reasons for making sure that, in the appropriate circumstances, we act out of motives of empathy and care. If we are to achieve our own goals, we must develop dispositions and patterns of thought and feeling in which we act out of consideration for the interests of others for their own sake. This is what I called economy-size altruism above. Success in life requires that we be able to take the interests of others seriously while allowing our own interests to slide into the background of our attention.

One might object here by pointing out that even when I am attending to the interests of others, my self-interest is playing a role encouraging me to act on motives of genuine care. But this generalized need to co-operate and sustain relationships is not appropriately described as egoism, because the primary motive and the object of my intention is the good of others. When the object of my intention is someone else's good, my action cannot be characterized as a selfish act, although there may be self-interested motives operating in the background. As I noted above, we are complicated beings with mixed motives.

Of course, none of this suggests that we should never have selfish motives or that we should always be rigorously sincere about our motives. Social interactions are complex and require varying degrees of self-interest and sincerity, and self-interest is one of our most powerful and effective motives. But if social interactions are to be successful we must maintain some capacity for taking the interests of others seriously.

The ethical egoist still has one more objection in her arsenal. I have been arguing that the need for co-operation in successful relationships requires that we have the ability to act for the benefit of others. But this seems to leave us with the conclusion that the less I need to co-operate with others, the less I need to treat them well. One might conclude that the best advice is to become as independent of other people as possible in order to avoid moral entanglements. In response to my claim that the egoist is unlikely to have successful relationships, an egoist might argue that relationships are overrated precisely because they prevent us from acting on our self-interest. A life lived independently, as much as possible avoiding the constraining influence of others, may be the ultimate refuge of egoism.

Most human beings would probably find such a life unrewarding, so egoism may at best be a philosophy that only a few individuals can endorse. Nevertheless, this objection deserves a response, which

I will give below when I have developed a richer account of moral agency.

We have been exploring the claim that to be capable of moral agency is to have certain interests or purposes that co-operation with others can advance. We have seen that although these interests and purposes are related to the self, we must be able to attend to the interests of others as well in ways that allow our self-interest to slip into the background as a secondary consideration. Thus, self-interest as a dominant motive does not explain our capacity for moral agency. Moral agency is better explained by our need to be reliable co-operators.

However, although our need to co-operate with others surely accounts for a large part of our capacity for moral agency, it does not provide a complete account. Many situations arise in life in which co-operation is not an issue. We do not depend on everyone we encounter and we could surely get away with treating them badly without cost to our ability to co-operate with those on whom we do depend. Thus, the need to co-operate does not explain our capacity or willingness to act well towards those on whom we do not depend.

Moreover, the fact that co-operation requires that we take the interests of others seriously falls far short of explaining the motivation of super-size altruism. Schindler did not merely take the interests of others seriously but risked sacrificing his wellbeing in favour of the interests of others. As I suggested above, it is likely that most human beings have some capacity for super-size altruism – at least in certain circumstances we will put the interests of others ahead of our own even when we receive no benefit and may even be harmed by our actions. Sometimes morality seems to require this of us. It may be the case that sometimes morality requires us to tell the truth, keep promises, act with a reasonable degree of benevolence towards others, etc, even when our own interests may be seriously harmed.

Yet, super-size altruism, because it involves no self-interest and may in fact require we sacrifice our interests, is puzzling as a component of moral agency. As I noted at the beginning of this chapter, intelligible action seems to require a purpose of some sort. I act because I want to achieve a goal. But how does altruistic action achieve a goal of mine? How can the interests of someone else become a reason for me to act if I do not share that interest?

MORAL AUTONOMY AND MORAL MOTIVES

In the history of philosophy, the eighteenth-century German philosopher Immanuel Kant supplied an important and influential answer to this question of how the interests of others can become a reason for me to act. Kant's account is not an explanation of altruism because he does not explain how we share the interests of others; rather his is an account of what it means to respect the interests of others.

According to Kant, moral requirements give me a reason to act because I impose them on myself. The reasons I have for acting morally must be my reasons and issue from my deliberation. Kant insisted that morality could not be imposed on us from outside. Neither God nor nature, let alone other persons, can impose a moral requirement on me.

This is because the source of human dignity is our capacity for freedom. We are distinguished from all other beings by our capacity to rationally choose our actions. If God, nature or other persons imposed moral requirements on us, against our will, our freedom would be fatally compromised. What is more, if our moral decisions were not free but imposed on us, we would not be morally responsible for them, thus undermining the system of praise and blame that is central to our moral framework. Thus, according to Kant, the basic condition for moral agency is moral autonomy – the capacity that each of us has to impose moral constraints on ourselves.

Thus far, Kant's thrilling praise of moral freedom seems compatible with ethical egoism. If moral decisions are up to me then it would seem that I am free to choose in accordance with my self-interest. However, Kant goes on to argue that I cannot achieve moral autonomy if desires, emotions and inclinations govern my moral judgements. Kant was convinced that nature is a mechanical system governed by deterministic, physical laws – causal relationships determine the behaviour of plants, animals and inanimate objects. They have no capacity to choose. But human desires, emotions and inclinations are also part of that deterministic universe, since they are a function of our bodily nature. When we act in accordance with desires, emotions and inclinations, we are simply responding to physical urges much as an animal does.

How can human beings escape this deterministic physical world? The only way we can exercise our freedom and autonomy is to rationally assess our actions independently of our desires. Moral reasoning will set us free – free from desires and emotions that chain us to nature. In contexts where moral judgement is required, by reasoning independently of desires, I am imposing moral principles on myself. My actions are self-directed rather than caused by external forces.

Kant is not arguing that we should never act on our desires or inclinations. In fact, most of the time we act on what he calls hypothetical imperatives, which involve desires. 'If you want to earn money, go to work.' 'If you are afraid of tigers, then stay out of the jungle.' These are perfectly acceptable as a basis for action. Actions based on these hypothetical imperatives have instrumental value – they get us something we want. But such actions have no moral value. When our actions reflect only our desires and inclinations, and not our capacity for moral reason, they are not free and thus they have no moral worth, since morality requires freedom.

Because Kant views emotions, desires and inclinations as deterministic causes of my actions, I don't deserve any moral credit when they motivate me to act since, in effect, I didn't choose my action. I become free to choose only through my use of reason to decide what to do. Thus for Kant, the requirements of morality are derived from the fact that human beings are free beings and can exercise that freedom only through moral reasoning.

Notice that Kant has fundamentally shifted the basis of moral agency away from the assumption I made at the beginning of this chapter. I said that the most natural way to understand human action in general is that an action is motivated by a purpose or interest that we have in a certain outcome. I eat because I have an interest in satisfying my hunger – satisfying my hunger is the purpose of my eating. I suggested that we understand moral action in the same way – as satisfying a purpose or interest. But if Kant is right that desires and inclinations are not appropriate moral motives, then how can morality satisfy an interest or purpose?

Kant's answer is that morality does not serve an interest or purpose. Morality is not about getting what we want or realizing a goal, not even the goal of freedom since freedom is what we are, not what we want. Morality is about exercising our capacity to choose freely, a capacity that is disrupted if we allow our wants to overwhelm our reasoning. According to Kant, the only proper moral motive is a demand I impose on myself to do what is right as reason dictates.

Kant refers to this motive as respect for the moral law. Thus, if I tell the truth because I am afraid of the consequences of being caught in a lie, I am not acting on a genuine moral motive for Kant. I am simply being cautious or fearful. I am, like an animal, satisfying desires and inclinations. If I help someone in desperate need of money out of sympathy for her plight, this is not a genuine moral motive either. I am acting from emotion. However, if I tell the truth or render assistance simply because rationality dictates it is the right thing to do, then I am acting on a genuine moral motive. I should emphasize that Kant is not claiming we should avoid sympathy or caution – both may help us perform moral duties. He is simply claiming that sympathy and caution have no moral worth.

Kant captures an important sentiment that is common in our ordinary moral discourse. When we accuse someone of wrongdoing, the fact she was doing what she wanted is not an excuse. People often say of someone in difficult circumstances, 'it is time for them to step up and do what is right'. This advice is pointing out that sometimes morality requires that we follow a moral principle despite the fact that doing so may harm our own interests or desires.

Kant does not provide an account of altruism because of the limited motives he considers genuinely moral. However, he does attempt to explain how certain interests that others have can play a substantial role in human action because, out of respect for the moral law, we can set aside our interests and desires and act impartially. For Kant, all human beings have this capacity because we have the capacity for freedom and reason, though we often fail to exercise it. Although Kant would not have put it this way, we might say that acting self-interestedly is not our most fundamental motive. Rather it is acting out of respect for our freedom or moral autonomy, which requires respect for the moral law. Only such an outlook acknowledges the fundamental fact of human freedom and accounts for the practice of holding people responsible for their actions. In summary, for Kant moral agency is the capacity to formulate and impose on oneself the moral law and to respect that ability in others.

Of course, Kant must still tell us what this moral law is and what it directs us to do. We will go into this on much more detail in the next chapter, but a brief discussion of Kant's conception of moral reasoning is necessary to evaluate Kant's conception of autonomy. Kant argues that when we suspend our desires and reason impartially about moral questions, the conditions under which human beings would see things differently are no longer in play. We can now look at matters objectively. And when we do so, we arrive at a single principle that captures this objectivity, which he calls the categorical imperative. In brief, the categorical imperative tells us never to use other people merely to satisfy our own ends (see Chapter 2 for a more detailed account). This principle simply follows from the human condition as Kant has described it. Human dignity is based on our capacity for freedom. We secure that freedom by a form of reason that suspends desires, emotions and inclinations. Once we have suspended our desires, the categorical imperative best captures the basic principle on which we must act. All rational beings will come to the same conclusion about the content of the moral law. The important point is that, according to Kant, our capacity for autonomy is fundamental to our capacity for moral agency, and this requires the capacity for impartiality – we must acknowledge moral constraints on our actions, independently of our wants or desires.

At this point, you might be puzzled by Kant's claim that 'morality expresses human freedom'. You might be asking 'How can I be free when morality requires me to forget about my wants and desires and impose rules on myself?' Especially when those rules are the same ones self-imposed by every other rational being. Again, Kant is trying to articulate an intuitively appealing idea. Part of what it means to be free or autonomous is to have self-control. People who act indiscriminately on any desire they have without thinking about whether it is really what they want, or whose emotional responses to situations are wildly inappropriate, are not free or independent. Instead, life is out of their control. They are at the mercy of whatever burden life imposes on them, and are easily manipulated by others into doing things they do not want to do. By contrast, a person who is self-directed sets goals and standards for herself, and is thus able to regulate her desires and emotions. Kant seems to be on the right track in arguing that freedom requires this ability to rationally set for ourselves the standards to which our lives ought to conform. Otherwise, we would be subject to external control, which would undermine our dignity as persons and our moral responsibility.

This idea of moral autonomy has been enormously influential, not only in philosophy, but in the moral framework of Western culture as well. It attempts to provide a foundation for a number of intuitions most of us would recognize as being distinctly moral. Beliefs such as that everyone should be treated with respect since all persons have the capacity for freedom and reason, that we should be fair and impartial when judging the actions of others as well as our own, and that moral rules apply to everyone without exception are a direct consequence of Kant's view.

However, it is not obvious that Kant has provided a coherent foundation for this idea of autonomy. Few philosophers have been convinced that we can adequately conceptualize freedom and autonomy without some reference to desires, goals and purposes. After all, freedom and autonomy are important to us, not only because it a source of human dignity, but because we care about whether we are free enough to satisfy our goals and desires. Kant does not think that the satisfaction of goals and desires is an essential component of freedom. But it is difficult to endorse such a view.

Furthermore, most contemporary philosophers reject the idea that desires and emotions necessarily interfere with our free will. Contemporary theories of the mind and of rationality tend to view reason and affective states such as desire and emotion as mutually dependent phenomena. Our capacity to reason is dependent on states of feeling and desire just as our feelings, if they are to give us reliable information about how we are situated in the world, must be based on rational beliefs. Freedom and autonomy is a matter of having control over emotions and desires, not reasoning independently of them.

Finally, there are doubts about whether respect for the moral law adequately explains our ability to be moral. It is obtuse to claim that when I sacrifice my interests to help someone who is suffering, my caring about them is not morally relevant; the only thing that matters is my respect for her capacity to formulate for herself the moral law. I doubt that caregivers are solely motivated by the thought that the person they care for is capable of being impartial. There is more to value in a human being than that! It is more plausible perhaps to claim that when I tell the truth I do so out of respect for the autonomy of the person to whom I am telling the truth, since a lie interferes with her freedom to make her own decisions. But in that case, I respect her general capacity as a free being to make decisions and act on them, not necessarily her capacity to formulate a moral principle for herself.

Thus, Kant has not identified the motives that explain the moral behaviour of most human beings. Of course, Kant does not see his task as that of explaining human behaviour. Kant is describing the motives of an ideal rational agent and encouraging actual human beings to aspire to that ideal as much as possible. But if there is so little connection between ideal rational agents and actual human beings, it is not obvious why we should take Kant's advice on this.

There is a deeper problem with Kant's view of moral motivation. Why would I bother to formulate the moral law for myself unless I were already predisposed to care about such things – unless I thought that morality played some essential role in human life and at least in a broad sense served some purpose that I have? The picture of human agency I began with seems inescapable. When we act, we aim to produce a result with our action. Our desire or interest in an outcome explains why we act. Without the desire, interest or purpose, it is hard to see why the action is intelligible. Yet, Kant denies that such factors can be genuine moral motives. Thus, Kant's recommendations seem disconnected from the lives of actual human beings. Yet, the idea that freedom is essential to moral agency is on the right track, if we can formulate it in a way that avoids Kant's implausible view on moral motivation.

PROCEDURAL AUTONOMY

Since Kant, there have been many reformulations of moral autonomy that attempt to avoid some of these objections. I will refer to these reformulations under the general heading of procedural autonomy. Advocates of procedural autonomy agree with Kant that a person can be a fully responsible moral agent only if she is capable of independent thought and action and can thus live in accordance with beliefs that she has adopted. But they disagree with Kant's view that a person can be autonomous only if her reasoning is impartial and independent of desires, emotions and inclinations. Desires and emotions inhibit autonomy only if they are in conflict with what a person really wants, or if they are the result of manipulation or coercion by forces outside a person's control. Thus, a person achieves procedural autonomy if she critically evaluates her beliefs and desires, and she endorses them without excessive interference by external authority. In other words, if the beliefs and desires that generate your actions are a sincere expression of your deepest values, and you settle on these values after sufficient deliberation, then you are autonomous. This is what it means to make one's own decisions, to be a self-directed person.

The nature of this deliberation and critical reflection is a matter of some disagreement, but most philosophers who endorse this view will not require the kind of objectivity and impartiality on which Kant insisted. An objective moral judgement is a judgement that is impartial because anyone can recognize its correctness independently of her point of view or circumstances. By contrast, the independence and freedom from interference that constitute the idea of autonomy are based on the idea that our actions should express our distinctive, individual points of view. Thus, autonomy and objectivity seem to be pulling in opposing directions. Nevertheless, most accounts of autonomy insist on some standards of rationality because reason is one of the capacities that enable us to be independent. We will discuss the requirements for reason in more detail in the next two chapters. For now, it will suffice to say that as long as we evaluate our beliefs and desires honestly and critically, choose effective means for accomplishing our goals, and reason consistently, the requirements of rationality are satisfied.

Philosopher Harry Frankfurt's version of procedural autonomy has been perhaps the most influential alternative to Kant's. On Frankfurt's view, it is important that an autonomous individual satisfy at least some of her desires. However, our desires are not equally important. We have immediate desires in practical situations that directly motivate us to act – a desire to eat, take a vacation from work, ask someone on a date, etc. These are first-order desires. But according to Frankfurt, we also have second-order desires that evaluate our first-order desires. Thus, for instance, I may have a first-order desire to take in a jazz concert this weekend and a second-order desire that my first-order desire be effective. I not only have the desire but I identify with it and want to make it part of my self. By contrast, last night at dinner I had a first-order desire for a second piece of cheesecake. But I didn't want to be motivated by that desire. I had a second-order desire not to be motivated by that first-order desire since I want to maintain healthy eating habits.

A person is autonomous when she identifies with her desires – when her lower-order desires are consistent with her higher-order values and principles and she reflects critically on her desires and values and approves of having them. Thus, it does not matter what our desires are, we are autonomous if we have thought about them and approve of them. An action is autonomous as long as it is the product of the agent's assessment of her situation rather than an unthinking, passive or coerced response. It is this active assessment that enables the agent to 'own' her actions.

Procedural autonomy is a plausible account of autonomy because it describes at least some of the psychological factors at work in sustaining our independence and freedom. Procedural autonomy also deepens our understanding of moral agency because it points to the importance of character in explaining the factors that enable people to act well. We can be genuinely free only if we get our desires to conform to our 'best self' – the person we really want to be.

However, procedural autonomy is limited as an account of moral agency. The problem is that procedural autonomy does not provide any content to the idea of second-order desires or what I called above the 'best self'. There is no requirement that the 'best self' includes moral values or that it be capable of putting the interests of others ahead of one's own interests. In other words, there seems to be no reason why an egoist could not be autonomous on this view. For a cinematic example of such a person, think of Hannibal Lecter, the character played by Anthony Hopkins in *The Silence of the Lambs*. A thoughtful and independent individual whose first-order desires conformed all to well to his deepest values! Thus, procedural autonomy does not provide enough content to our basic values to get moral agency off the ground.

In summary, the Kantian view of autonomy was unable to explain our motives to be moral. Procedural autonomy is compatible with genuine moral motives but it fails to provide any content to morality or require such motives. Neither provides an adequate account of moral agency.

RELATIONAL AUTONOMY

There is a third option that is the product of recent work done by feminist philosophers with an interest in showing that our traditional notions of autonomy are misguided. This third approach is called relational autonomy. We can define relational autonomy as the view that our capacity to be self-directed (as defined according to procedural autonomy) is dependent on our ability to enter into and sustain a variety of relationships. As social beings, each of us develops the capacity for autonomy through social interaction. My capacity to choose the kind of life I want to lead or the person I want to be can neither be acquired nor exercised by myself.

Relationships enable autonomy in two ways. First, relationships with parents, teachers, friends, co-workers and others enable us to acquire the ability to act independently as we develop into adults; and these relationships help to sustain autonomy throughout our lives since most human beings remain connected to communities of various sorts. The social and cultural institutions of the various communities we are part of provide us with the means through which we sustain autonomy. To be able to make our own choices we need political liberties, information, education, good health, financial resources and protection from a variety of threats, all of which social institutions and relationships provide.

Second, the social contexts in which we live constitute our self-conceptions as autonomous persons. Part of being self-directed is to see oneself in that way. How we see ourselves is as much a product of feedback from others as it is a self-generated perception. Furthermore, our social context helps to construct the way we as individuals define autonomy and the value it has for us. The kinds of choices we have, how we go about making them and acting on them, the significance we attach to our goals and projects, the significance we attach to our ability to control the circumstances of life, are all penetrated by social understandings. We understand our characteristics, goals and inclinations, in part, as others in our society or culture view them. Moreover, most of our goals and aspirations are shared goals and aspirations. We can choose them and act on those decisions only in collaboration with others.

This, of course, does not mean that we cannot reject certain aspects of our social conditioning. We can evaluate, modify or reject many aspects of this social conditioning, but in that process of development we are relying on capabilities that we acquire and sustain through socialization as well. The critical reflection that we use to reject aspects of our socialization is itself enabled by that socialization.

Think about the abilities that enable you to reject some of what your parents taught you, adopt values in conflict with social norms, resist peer pressure, block the influence of media manipulation, and recognize that some of your desires may not be appropriate for you to act on, etc. Your ability to resist unwanted external influence requires political freedom, knowledge and understanding, imagination, self-respect and motivation. We cannot acquire or sustain any of these on our own.

There is a third sense in which autonomy is relational. Autonomy is valuable to us because we want our decisions and actions to express our subjectivity – our unique, individual points of view. However, the things we care about make up that individual point of view. My individuality is in part a product of the things I care about, and I value my point of view because it is permeated with things of value. Unless we are thoroughly narcissistic, we care about things other than ourselves. My point of view is, in part, constructed out of my caring for my wife, daughter, philosophy, music, etc. Thus, the exercise of autonomy depends on sustaining our caring responses to what we love. We want freedom and independence so that we are free to care about what matters to us. If this were not the case, the exercise of autonomy would be an empty gesture.

When our autonomy is disrupted, we can see clearly the degree to which autonomy is dependent on what we care about. The loss of autonomy is painful because we are no longer free to care as we did before the disruption. For instance, if a husband forbids his wife to continue working at a job she enjoys, she has not merely lost some of her freedom, she has lost the ability to be motivated by something she cares about.

Relational autonomy seems at first to be a paradoxical idea. Autonomy is about independence. How can my independence be possible only through greater dependence on others? An example will help clarify matters. Imagine that Glenn is an able but ruthless businessman who climbs the corporate ladder stabbing people in the back along the way, and bending and breaking corporate rules and regulations to get to the top. He is talented and politically savvy enough to be successful – he has power and independence. Along the way, though, he has to enlist many people in his schemes, so he is in this position because of relationships. Superior educational opportunities and a genetic endowment supply him with the intelligence, drive and charm that enable him to succeed. His definition of success, the very existence of his company, the legal and regulatory framework that he takes advantage of, are the product of an institutional context on which he is thoroughly dependent. Furthermore, he is now a slave to the rhythms of a crushing work schedule made necessary in part because he must keep an eye on everything – his backstabbing and raw ambition means that no one trusts him and he can't trust anyone else. Now that he is on top, he will need protection, information and co-operation from others. But if he has damaged his relationships, he will spend most of his time fending off challenges without the ability to trust anyone around him. He is now utterly dependent on enforcers, snitches and spies, and his ability to make others fear him. Importantly, if he cares only for his career, salary and stock options, but not about his company, customers or investors, the company in the end will be inefficient, and lack enough human and material resources to do what it is supposed to do well. Because he is thoroughly dependent on market forces for his survival the prospects of his firm will more than likely decline. The firm will be broken up and sold off and he will now depend on the ability of public relations people to burnish his reputation and hide his deficiencies so he can compete for the next job.

Now, of course, there are people like this, and sometimes they become successful. Nevertheless, they fail to achieve independence. Independence from relationships is an illusion, and any realistic account of independence must make reference to relationships. Autonomy is not a matter of achieving independence from others. Rather, it involves finding ways of depending on others that are compatible with our integrity and the ability to control our lives.

More importantly for our purposes in this chapter, relational autonomy clarifies the nature of moral agency because it promises a solution to the problem of procedural autonomy noted above. Recall that, on the procedural view, an agent has autonomy if she reflectively endorses her first-order desires in light of her deeper values and commitments. The problem with procedural autonomy was that, because it does not specify any substantive value commitments that an autonomous agent must have, it could not provide a foundation for moral agency. A consistent moral egoist could be autonomous in the procedural sense. However, on the relational view of autonomy we can see at least the broad outlines of substantive moral commitments that are required in order to be autonomous.

Relational autonomy adds to the procedural view the idea that our deepest values and commitments must be directed towards entering into and sustaining relationships, since without them the achievement of autonomy is impossible. Procedural autonomy asserts that a person is autonomous if her lower-order desires are consistent with her higher-order values and she reflects critically on her desires and values and approves of having them. Relational autonomy agrees but adds that a person must also seek to sustain the relationships on which her autonomy depends. Thus, relational autonomy begins to explain our capacity for moral agency, as well as our interest in it, because in order to enter into and sustain the relationships necessary for autonomy one must adopt and act on a moral point of view.

In summary, in order to be an agent and act effectively with purpose in the world, I must be autonomous. I must make my own decisions and they must be compatible with my deepest desires and values. In order to be autonomous, I must enter into and sustain relationships. The intelligibility of and capacity for autonomy requires relationships. In order to enter into and sustain relationships I must be a moral agent with the capacity to act from a moral point of view. Morality requires freedom (in the sense of autonomy), but freedom requires morality as well.

The idea of relational autonomy solves a variety of problems that have arisen in this discussion of moral agency. Relational autonomy begins the process of clarifying the purpose of morality – morality enables us to enter into and sustain relationships that contribute to our functioning and flourishing in the world as autonomous beings. Thus, moral motives are compatible with the most plausible view of human agency in which our actions are goal-directed. Relational autonomy also provides part of the explanation for how the interests of others can be a reason for me to act even when I do not share their interest. To see this, we have to build in more structure to the idea of relational autonomy.

To have autonomy is to be self-directed. It is to be in a position whereby my actions reflect my own beliefs and desires. To achieve autonomy we must be capable of a pattern of deliberation in which we assess desires and values as well as our situations, including relationships, in order to exert the requisite control over our lives. However, this pattern of deliberation must cover not only the past and present but the future as well. Much of our ability to control factors in our lives involves the way we anticipate the future. If we anticipate the future in a way that excessively closes down possibilities and makes it more difficult to make decisions and act on them in the future, then we suffer a loss of autonomy. But of course the future is unpredictable. Although we can make some rough predictions based on our past and present, we cannot reliably predict what beliefs and desires we may have in the future, the kinds of obstacles we will confront, or the kinds of relationships we will have to enter into. Thus, in order to maintain control over our lives we have to be open to new possibilities, to be ready to revise plans, take advantage of opportunities, acquire new skills, new interests, and most importantly enter into new relationships. Whatever the future is going to be for each of us, it will be a future entered into with others, in which relationships of dependence will be crucial to our ability to maintain control over our lives. But that means that we have to develop dispositions to respond to people in ways that sustain the possibility of relationship.

I will discuss these dispositions in more detail in later chapters. For now it will be sufficient to point to qualities of character like the ability to treat people with fairness and respect, honesty, kindness, etc. Importantly, these are not dispositions that can be turned on or off at will. As discussed above, to be effective our motives must be reasonably consistent and embedded in our psychologies in a way that enables us to be naturally responsive, a matter of habit. By 'habit,' I do not mean a tendency to act without thinking; I mean a tendency to consistently respond appropriately according to what the situation demands. Thus, we cannot treat well only those on whom we already depend, but must also treat with respect those with whom we have a potential relationship as well. The dispositions of personality and character required to sustain an openness to the future encourage us to treat people well even when we do not share their interest. Since the future is open and indeterminate, we do not know whether we share their interests or not. And even if we have good evidence that we don't share a common interest, in the absence of a threat or an offense of some sort, a person concerned to maximize control over her life will not shut down those dispositions that enable us to enter into and sustain relationships. Thus, relational autonomy requires a conception of moral agency that explains not only moral acts directed towards familiar others, but also moral acts directed towards strangers.

To avoid misunderstanding, two points must be emphasized. First, we have an account of what motivates moral agents and what makes moral conduct, including altruistic actions, intelligible to moral agents. We have not yet addressed the question of which specific actions are justified or obligatory. We have an account of the capacity and motivation to treat strangers well, but as yet no account of what kinds of treatment are morally required, or when we are justified in suspending these motives. These issues are not strictly speaking questions of moral agency but of moral justification and will be discussed in subsequent chapters.

Second, I do not want to suggest that all relationships are worthwhile or that all relationships enhance autonomy. Clearly, some relationships are destructive or irrelevant, and most relationships introduce conflicts that are difficult and perhaps impossible to resolve. A significant aspect of the achievement of autonomy is the capacity to maintain integrity despite persistent conflict. Chapter 6 includes a discussion of this point.

This account of moral agency sets aside the remaining response of the egoist who might claim that, because the less dependent I am on others the less moral I need to be, one ought to pursue a life devoted to being as independent as possible. As we have seen, independence is itself dependent on relationships. Thus, we are unlikely to preserve that independence by acting only on our self-interest. A life devoted to separating oneself from others in order to maintain the ability to act only on one's self-interest may be a possible life for human beings. But it is a crabbed and meagre life devoid of the goods that most human beings seek.

Finally, relational autonomy begins to make Schindler's actions intelligible, although the details of this account must be filled in later when we have a richer conceptual apparatus in place. It is plausible to argue that Schindler's ability to respond to the needs of his workers rested on his relationship with them. They were vulnerable; he was their protector and no one else was in a position to help them. Schindler's sense of his own independence and control demanded of him that he take on the burden of their rescue. I doubt that Schindler would have given such assistance to anyone at any time. Those workers in that situation at that time provoked his heroic response.

REFERENCES AND SUGGESTIONS FOR FURTHER READING

Dworkin, Gerald (1988), *The Theory and Practice of Autonomy*, Cambridge: Cambridge University Press.

Frankfurt, Harry G. (1987), 'Identification and Wholeheartedness', in *Responsibility, Character and the Emotions*, ed. F. Schoeman, Cambridge: Cambridge University Press.

Kant, Immanuel (1964) [1785], *Groundwork of the Metaphysics of Morals*, trans. H.J. Paton, New York: Harper and Row.

Mackenzie, Catriona, and Stoljar, Natalie (eds.) (2000), *Relational Autonomy*, Oxford: Oxford University Press.

CHAPTER 2

OBJECTIVE MORAL REASONS

The conception of moral agency developed in Chapter 1 requires that reason plays a significant role in our ability to be in control of our lives. We have to reason about what our goals should be and reason about the best way of accomplishing them. Furthermore, the ability to reason critically about our desires helps us to maintain our autonomy by assessing desires in light of more deeply held values and commitments.

However, reasons play another role as well. To participate in a network of relationships that make up our system of co-operation we have to be able to give reasons for our actions when called upon to do so. When our actions affect others, the people affected are likely to ask us to justify our actions, not only with respect to their effectiveness or efficiency, but from a moral point of view as well. Our ability to participate in that system of co-operation depends on our ability to supply an adequate justification for what we plan to do or have done. Because these will be reasons that others must accept or reject, not just any reason will count. There are good reasons and bad reasons and to sort them out we need to develop standards of acceptability for our reasons. This chapter is about various attempts to develop standards of acceptability for moral reasons.

When we justify our actions in ordinary contexts, we often make judgements that are supported by widely accepted standards of behaviour called moral norms. For instance, a librarian can justify fining me for not returning a book on time because it is a widely accepted norm, supported by sanctions, that borrowers should return books on or before the due date. However, if our actions are to be justified, the norms we use to justify them must themselves be justifiable. The fact that a norm is widely accepted does not make it correct. What justifies norms such as stealing is wrong, one should not lie, etc.? A philosophical account of moral reasoning must answer this question.

Most traditional accounts of moral reasoning assert that moral reasons must be objective. Recall from Chapter 1 that 'objective' means unbiased and impartial. An objective reason is not based on my point of view or your point of view but rests on independent considerations. If we can rest moral judgements on objective reasons then moral judgements will be stable since they will not shift depending on your point of view or my point of view. They will represent common ground that we all share. In Chapter 1, I argued that our motives for acting morally cannot be impartial. In this chapter, I am asking a somewhat different question. Can our reasons for acting be impartial?

In part, the reason for insisting on the objectivity of moral reasons arises from worries about relativism. Thus, we will look at relativism first before turning directly to a discussion of objectivity.

RELATIVISM

One very popular view has it that the standards of acceptability for a moral judgement are dependent on one's culture or social group. This view is called moral relativism, and it gets its plausibility from the fact that cultures or social groups appear to have very different norms by which they live. From the standpoint of radical Islam, the terrorist attacks of September 11 are morally justified. From the standpoint of most of us in Western society, they are not. In certain countries or tribes in Africa, genital mutilation of young girls is an acceptable way of enforcing sexual mores; in much of the rest of the world, it is not. Throughout history, in many parts of the world, elderly persons who were no longer productive were expected to commit suicide. We think such an expectation is cruel.

The diversity of moral codes that exist today as well as throughout history indicates that there is no single morality that governs all human beings. As an empirical fact, this claim seems obviously true. However, moral relativism takes this empirical claim one step further. Not only do different social groups in fact follow different norms, they should follow different norms because no independent standards exist that allow us to determine which set of norms is correct. An action is right or wrong only relative to the norms of particular social groups. Thus, to say that an action is wrong is simply to say that the dominant norms of a particular group forbid it.

Moral relativism is a controversial position because many people are disturbed by the possibility that an action may be morally wrong in one society but permissible in another society. These worries are exacerbated by the possibility that relativism might apply to smaller groups within society as well, so that what is wrong for you might not be wrong for your neighbour. Even more disturbing is the fact that relativism forbids important judgements that are central to our sense of who we are. For instance, today most people in our society condemn the genocidal anti-Semitism of Nazism, and this condemnation is essential to our moral point of view. Yet, if relativism is true, this judgement is not rational because there is no independent standard of justification that would show this judgement to be correct. Relativism seems to rule out criticism of anyone outside one's own culture or subculture.

This does not mean that relativism rules out all forms of criticism. Relativism is compatible with internal criticism in which specific beliefs or practices are criticized for being dysfunctional or violating their own internal standards. A society can rationally criticize practices within its boundaries for being incompatible with the dominant norms of that society. Furthermore, relativism does not entail that anything is permissible. Social norms can be quite strict and require a great deal of conformity. The problem with relativism is not that anything is permitted; it is that the resources for criticism and justification are limited.

Let's examine some of the arguments for moral relativism. One argument in support of relativism is that the very fact there is such a diversity of moral beliefs means that there cannot be a single correct moral code. This argument by itself is not convincing. Obviously, some people have false beliefs about all kinds of things. Why cannot some moral beliefs be false? Scientists disagree vehemently about the causes of cancer, historians argue about the origins of revolutions, and economists disagree about how tax policy affects the economy. Yet, despite this diversity of opinion, some claims turn out to be true and others false. The mere fact of diversity entails nothing about the truth of the different beliefs. Some social groups may simply be mistaken about what the correct moral code is.

Another argument for relativism is that if relativism is true we can be more tolerant and accepting of others. Once we see that our own way of life is no better from a moral point of view than other ways of life we should be less inclined to judge them, less inclined to get into conflicts with them, and more inclined to see the virtues of alternative ways of living. One problem with this view is that if criticism of other cultures is unjustifiable, then approval of other cultures is equally without foundation. But there is a deeper problem with this view – it produces a practical contradiction. Suppose the relativist confronts an intolerant culture whose members adhere rigidly to their views with conviction. The relativist cannot claim that this intolerance is not justified – she has no principle outside her own beliefs to justify her claim. She cannot advocate that everyone ought to be tolerant since relativism denies the possibility of defending this sort of universal claim. Thus, she must tolerate the intolerant. But if there is real conflict here and the intolerant views are being forced on the relativist she is faced with the dilemma of either failing to defend her position that relativism is true for her, or violating her principle of tolerance by fighting back against the intolerant. In a world where competing moral visions persistently come into conflict, relativism does not look like a promising position.

There is, however, a more sophisticated argument for relativism. This argument rests on the plausible claim that the only way to acquire a set of moral beliefs is to acquire them through socialization within a particular social group. The social groups in which we live determine our values and desires because these values and desires are, after all, responses to the conditions under which we live. Thus, there is no way to make a moral decision independently of this framework, because the tools we need to make such decisions are deeply embedded in this way of life. No alternative form of life can ever seem quite so compelling and reasons that arise from alternative ways of living cannot have a purchase on us.

This is a very compelling argument for relativism because it rests on the plausible claim that facts about the conditions under which people live generate their moral beliefs. Morality consists of the norms that a people adopt in order to overcome obstacles to their flourishing and preserve social order. Thus, moral beliefs are acquired under a particular set of physical constraints and social conditions, and the reasons they have for justifying their norms will seem compelling only to those who share a condition. They will not seem compelling to someone who faces different obstacles and is nourished by different traditions.

Although this is a plausible account of how we acquire moral norms, as an argument for relativism it is subject to two objections. The first is that this argument assumes that cultures or subcultures must be relatively isolated so that we can never acquire enough familiarity with others to make judgements about their moral practices. This may have been the case before modern forms of communication and transportation made contact between disparate cultures possible. I doubt that in most cases it is true today. It may require a great deal of empathy and imagination to acquire enough understanding of others to make informed judgements about them. But it is not impossible. Understanding is a matter of degree and we need not possess complete understanding of something before raising questions about it. In a global culture, the distinction between being inside a culture vs. outside a culture is highly contested and no longer provides stable ground by which to rule out critical perspectives.

The mistake the relativist makes here is to assume that a particular moral belief or practice is so tightly wedded to the conditions under which it emerged that we are unable to view it from any other aspect. Given the fact of rapid social change, the question of whether a belief continues to serve a purpose or not is always intelligible and can be raised from a variety of perspectives within and outside a social group. In other words, we are not positioned so fully within a culture or tradition that we cannot grasp alternatives with some degree of understanding.

Furthermore, if certain beliefs acquired their support based on facts that turn out to be false, then their being part of a cultural tradition is irrelevant to their evaluation. Such beliefs warrant criticism regardless of how deeply embedded in a culture a belief is. For instance, many cultures discriminate against women in the workforce based on the belief that women are less intelligent than men are. They hold this belief despite the fact that scientific evidence shows that belief to be false. Similarly, Nazism was based on false beliefs about the superiority of the Aryan race, the influence of Jews on German culture and the reasons for Germany's diminished position in the world.

When cultures come into conflict in the global marketplace of ideas, each idea must be argued for and defended if it is to attract and maintain adherents. This acts as a constraint on any moral system that seeks to insulate itself from criticism. The most important constraint is the demand that factual claims require empirical evidence for their support. To the extent that any culture or subculture is part of a larger system of relationships – and as I suggested, today, most cultures are – they cannot ignore the demand to give reasons for their practices if they expect to remain a part of that system. Relationships impose these kinds of constraints on us.

The second objection to this argument for relativism is that, although each culture perhaps confronts unique obstacles, which their moral norms function to overcome, all human beings share a condition that requires a range of common responses. All cultures must produce and sustain enough wealth to survive, deal with the threat of mortality, solve communication and co-ordination problems, and raise their young. This means that the moral practices of all cultures will resemble each other in some respects. It is difficult to imagine a culture that has no rules against murder, no standards of honesty, and no norms governing the raising of children. A culture that lacked these would be unable to sustain itself for even a generation.

This suggests that we should adopt a position that philosopher Nina Rosenstand calls soft universalism. Soft universalism asserts that there are some basic moral principles that every culture shares, though each culture may apply these principles differently. Every culture may have rules against murder but there are vast differences regarding how those rules are applied, to whom they apply and what kinds of exceptions they permit. The fact that there are similarities in the obstacles that all human beings confront gives us a starting point for evaluating competing ways of overcoming those obstacles. We can talk about better and worse ways of confronting mortality, preserving the reliability of communication, etc.

However, although the relativist is wrong to suggest that there are no grounds for criticizing or evaluating other cultural practices, the relativist might be right that there is no single, correct moral code. From the fact that all claims can be criticized and we must defend them with reasons, it does not follow that there are clear criteria for resolving all moral disagreements. Though we may be able to show some moral codes are inferior because they are incompatible with facts or fail to solve the problems they are designed to solve, we may not be able to show that one and only one form of life is correct using these criteria. Consequently, there may exist many different ways of living with distinct, contrasting moral codes, and no criteria that would allow us to compare them. Although there may be a few, very general common principles that all these ways of life share, differences in how we weigh the relative worth of various goods may be so significant that the norms that express these principles may produce widely divergent, incompatible courses of action. For instance, though all cultures have norms that mitigate conflict and advance co-operation, the way in which we set the terms of co-operation may be vastly different. In Western culture, we place substantial value on autonomy and individuality. However, many cultures throughout the world value social cohesion, community and tradition more highly. There may exist no fact of the matter that demonstrates which is correct and no single criterion that would enable us to compare them.

This suggests an alternative to relativism, called value pluralism, and it has many of the virtues of relativism without its vices. Unlike relativism, value pluralism does not claim that all value systems are equally good or that we cannot criticize value systems. It is compatible with the view that some people may be mistaken about what is valuable and that some value systems are simply inadequate. However, it grants the existence of a variety of value systems that are compatible with living a good human life.

Pluralism is also compatible with what appear to be the empirical facts about moral differences. If we look at the variety of differences that characterize human sociality and the conflicts that arise because of those differences, it is reasonable to conclude that there are many different ways to live and no rational procedure for adjudicating all conflicts between them.

Value pluralism, however, leaves us with an unpalatable consequence. Because there are conflicts that cannot be rationally resolved, it seems to leave us with a stark choice between tolerance for views we find offensive or the use of force to resolve conflict. At the point where we need to rely on reason to resolve serious conflict, reason is impotent. Many philosophers have found this unacceptable. Thus, difficulties with moral relativism and pluralism have encouraged the search for a theory of moral reasoning that will be absolute and universal. We will now turn to an analysis of these theories.

MORAL REALISM

If reason is to be powerful enough to resolve conflicts between competing views of how to live, it must be able to supply a basis for reasoning that is independent of those competing views. Reasons to act must be such that anyone can see their point regardless of religious beliefs, cultural traditions or particular desires. In other words, moral reasons must be objective.

Thus far, I have defined an 'objective' reason as a reason that is impartial or unbiased. For some philosophers, in order for a judgement to be unbiased it must refer to something mind-independent. An objective judgement is a judgement that responds to factors that are external to the mind. But there are a variety of ways to understand what it means to be external to the mind. Some philosophers have suggested a view called moral realism. On this account, moral facts that are part of the external world guide objective moral judgements. Moral judgements are judgements about how the world is, and these judgements can be either true or false. Since 'how the world is' is independent of what we think about the world, judgements guided by how the world is are not products of a particular perspective but are objective.

However, moral realism has not received widespread acceptance because there seems to be an important distinction between facts and values. It is one thing to observe that 'Nathan is hurting John'. This is an observable fact. However, to state that 'Nathan's treatment of John is bad' is to assert something else. Not only am I stating that there is an event occurring, I am also assigning a value to it in claiming it is bad. In the first sentence, I am simply describing a state of affairs and, if my description is true, it is guided by how the world is. In the second sentence, I am prescribing an action, implicitly recommending that Nathan stop hurting John. In the statement 'Nathan's treatment of John is bad' I am not just perceiving reality, but projecting an attitude onto reality. The badness of Nathan's treatment of John is not something observable. The projection of my attitude is mind-dependent, a product of my mental state, not mind-independent. Thus, such a moral judgement is not objective.

The moral realist is sometimes accused of committing the naturalistic fallacy. The naturalistic fallacy names a mistake in reasoning that involves deducing what ought to be the case from what is the case. It is not obvious that all such derivations are fallacies. Presumably, a conception of what human beings ought to do must have some connection with facts about human nature. However, it is clear that deducing 'ought' statements from 'is' statements involves further argument, not a simple statement of the facts.

This debate over moral realism is complex, by no means settled, and takes many twists and turns, which we shall not follow here. For our purposes, it is sufficient to point out that basing objectivity on an analogy between ordinary facts and moral facts does not seem promising.

LOGICAL CONSISTENCY

An alternative approach to objectivity that has garnered more support is to view moral reasons, not as guided by facts about the world, but as guided by the binding force of logical consistency. The idea is that any rational being must conform to the principles of logic. Thus, if we can show as a matter of logic, that certain moral principles are justified, then the principles will be objectively valid for all rational beings. They are objective in the sense that they do not represent the perspective of this person or that person but are required of any rational being. They are mind-independent in the sense that they are independent of particular perspectives or interests.

This approach to demonstrating the objectivity of moral judgements has a variety of formulations. One of the more accessible is by Thomas Nagel who argues that, when we unpack a common response to wrongdoers – 'how would you like it if someone did that to you?' – we can see the objective basis of moral reasons. Nagel argues it is human nature to resent people who do not consider our interests. When someone intentionally harms me, I get angry with her for being inconsiderate. Thus, I think that other people have a reason to consider my interests. But I am no different from others who have interests. Their interests are just as important to them as my interests are to me.

Here is where the force of logical consistency enters the picture. It is a basic principle of reason that if a reason applies in one case, it applies in any case that is relevantly similar. To use a reason as justification for an action in one case, but then to withdraw that reason in another case that is similar in every relevant way, would be arbitrary and unmotivated. Rationality requires us to be consistent. Therefore, if others have a reason to consider my interests, given the requirement of logical consistency, I have a reason to consider their interests. Thus, considering everyone's interests is an objective and universal moral requirement.

Nagel concludes from this that all human beings are capable of impartial motivation. We can be moved to make moral judgements from a purely objective point of view. Of course, this motivation competes with other motives of a more selfish or personal nature. But justifying a particular action is a matter of considering reasons why we ought to act impartially, independently of personal motives, weighing them against our other motives.

Nagel's argument is powerful and appealing but it is limited in important ways. Notice that though he claims we always have a reason to consider the interests of others, we need not always act on that reason. Presumably, in any reasonably complex situation we have a variety of reasons to act – some of them may be self-interested reasons. Whether our self-interested reasons ought to override the interests of others in a particular situation is a question Nagel's argument does not answer.

Also, note that, according to Nagel, to be rational is to be consistent. However, although consistency may be an important aspect of rationality, it is certainly not the whole of it. It is also rational to pursue happiness, choose effective means of satisfying desires, etc., and these dimensions of rationality can come into conflict with consistency requirements. When being consistent conflicts with these other goals, it is not obvious that rationality requires absolute consistency. Nagel needs additional argument to demonstrate the supreme importance of consistency.

This brings us to a deeper problem, which I began to address in Chapter 1 but must be revisited in this discussion of moral reasons. Nagel assumes that if we have a reason to do something, that we also have a motive to do it. This is a highly contested issue in moral philosophy. Do reasons, by themselves, supply motives or must reasons be accompanied by desires in order to induce someone to act? I argued, in Chapter 1, that agency requires a motive, desire or purpose. But we need to explore the question of whether reason supplies its own motive in more detail. I will discuss this issue below, so keep in mind there is an important question that must be settled before we find Nagel's argument acceptable.

Nagel's purpose is to clarify the degree to which the meaning of ordinary moral claims requires a commitment to an objective point of view. However, even if we endorse Nagel's argument, we still have to know how, beginning with this objective point of view, we are to reason about moral questions. So let's assume for now that Nagel is correct about the necessity of the objective point of view, and turn to the question of what moral reasoning from an objective point of view looks like in detail by looking at the two main theories of moral reasoning and justification – utilitarianism and deontology.

UTILITARIANISM

When we evaluate an action, we can focus on various dimensions of the action. We can evaluate the person who is acting, the intention or motive of the person acting, the nature of the act itself, or the consequences. Consequentialism is the view that what makes an action right or wrong are its consequences. With regard to the evaluation of an act, the other dimensions of the action are not important. The most widely held consequentialist theory is utilitarianism.

Utilitarianism has a long and illustrious pedigree. It was first elaborated in detail by Jeremy Bentham in 1781. Since then, it has endured countless permutations in the hands of philosophers and economists attracted to its potential for social reform. Utilitarianism seeks to replace reliance on God, tradition, common sense or intuitions with reasoning about facts and their consequences.

Utilitarianism begins with a perception about human nature – human beings for the most part seek to improve their wellbeing. Therefore, our actions should promote wellbeing. There has been a good deal of dispute about what counts as wellbeing. The early utilitarians thought of it in terms of pleasure; many utilitarians today think of preference satisfaction as the ultimate good. However, there is good reason to think that neither pleasure nor preference satisfaction captures the range of things that human beings value. We will discuss the idea of wellbeing in more detail in Chapter 5. For now, we will assume that wellbeing includes the sort of things that most of us want – continued life, good health, food, shelter, loving relationships, education, etc.

Given that we all have an interest in our own wellbeing, the utilitarian argues that we should cause as much of it to exist as possible. But whose wellbeing should we promote? Like Nagel, utilitarianism argues that all of us have an equal interest in our own wellbeing. From an objective point of view, we must consider our own interest to be equal to the interests of everyone else. Thus, we should try to produce the greatest aggregate total wellbeing for everyone who will be affected by our actions. This can be captured in a single basic principle, called the principle of utility.

The principle of utility is as follows: 'Of the courses of action available, choose the one that produces the greatest aggregate wellbeing.' In other words, we take everyone affected by a contemplated action, determine how the action will effect them, add all these effects together, subtracting negative effects from positive effects, and compare that sum with the sum of the effects of alternative actions. We are obligated to choose the action that maximizes overall wellbeing. According to this version of utilitarianism, we are to evaluate each action we contemplate with regard to how it promotes the general welfare. Thus, we call this version act utilitarianism.

According to act utilitarianism, the principle of utility is the sole source of moral rightness. No action is right or good, regardless of its source, unless it conforms to the principle of utility. God's laws, traditional moral maxims, habits of character such as honesty, pangs of conscience, etc., produce right actions only if they are in accordance with the principle of utility.

Utilitarianism is a plausible theory of moral reasoning for two reasons: it is directed towards promoting the common good, something we probably don't do often enough; and it is clear that often our intuitive reasoning is utilitarian. The theory claims to be simply adding more rigour and precision to our common sense approach to reasoning. In countless situations everyday we contemplate what the consequences of our actions will be, and we choose the action that will produce the best consequences. The utilitarian argues that simply by clarifying what counts as a best consequence and specifying the kinds of reason that will produce the best consequence we can systematize all of our moral reasoning.

However, if utilitarianism is our only pattern of moral reasoning, we run into problems. The first set of problems has to do with making good on the claim that this is an objective way of evaluating our actions. Even though the utilitarian considers everyone's interests equally, how do we know what those interests are? How do we make interpersonal comparisons regarding what people value? Even if we agree on the kinds of things that human beings think are good – continued life, health, food, shelter, education, etc. – the relative value of each will differ from person to person. So how is a decision-maker to know which goods a diverse group of people will prefer?

Furthermore, to be precise in our calculations of wellbeing, we need to assign numerical value to various goods produced by the actions being considered. But how do we accurately assign numerical value to goods that differ in quality, not just quantity?

In our economic system, we solve both problems by allowing a free market to decide how to distribute goods. We replace the idea of wellbeing with preference satisfaction, and then allow the amount of money a person is willing to buy or sell a product for to determine the value things have. The problem with this as an objective way of determining the relative worth of the consequences of our actions is that many things we value are not market goods and cannot be assigned monetary value. What is the price of a human life, friendship, self-respect, freedom, etc.? Moreover, people who lack the resources to enter the market or the knowledge to make intelligent choices cannot express their preferences. Thus, in the end such a system does not consider everyone's interests equally. Economists and others who work in the area of public policy have complex formulas for trying to deal with these issues, but their resolution remains a thorny problem.

A second group of objections concerns the role of justice and rights within utilitarianism. The principle of utility says to maximize aggregate wellbeing. Suppose we could create massive wealth for society by enslaving a minority group. If society as a whole benefits enough from slavery, it would outweigh the negative consequences on the slaves. Such an action, then, would be justified according to the principle. However, according to common sense morality, we think that justice and fundamental rights for individuals are too important to be sacrificed for the common good. Individuals are not simply means to an end but are ends in themselves with their own interests and concerns. To treat persons only as means to an end is to deny the respect that persons deserve.

Act utilitarianism can grant the importance of rights and justice but only in cases where granting them produces more aggregate wellbeing. When rights and justice do not promote the common good, they should be ignored. However, the whole idea of a right is that it entitles the rights holder to certain kinds of treatment regardless of the consequences for society. Thus, utilitarianism is often criticized for ignoring justice and rights. The fundamental problem is that utilitarianism fails to take seriously the separateness of persons since it simply aggregates their welfare into a sum total and does not concern itself with how that welfare is distributed.

A third group of objections concerns the role of obligations.

Intuitively, actions such as respecting the property of others, telling the truth and keeping promises are important moral principles. However, act utilitarianism treats them as optional depending on the contingent matter of whether they have good consequences or not. Suppose for instance, I borrow $1,000 from a rich friend promising to pay him back in six months. When the time comes to pay him back, I could donate that $1,000 to charity and produce more aggregate wellbeing. After all, he is well off and doesn't really need $1,000. Intuitively I am obligated to keep my promise to pay him back. Utilitarianism says otherwise.

Finally, many criticize utilitarianism for being too demanding. In requiring that we always choose what is best for aggregate wellbeing, utilitarianism seems to leave little room for us to pursue personal projects and interests or care for our own lives.

Many advocates of utilitarianism refuse to shrink from these results and simply argue that our intuitions about rights and obligations are irrational holdovers from discredited moral systems. We should adopt utilitarianism despite these results. However, others have tried to answer these objections by developing alternative conceptions of utilitarianism. The most common variant is rule utilitarianism, sometimes referred to as indirect utilitarianism.

The difference between act utilitarianism and rule utilitarianism is the entity to which we apply the principle of utility. The act utilitarian says apply it to each action. The rule utilitarian says we should not consider each action separately because patterns of actions can have consequences as well. Thus, we should look at the type of action we are engaged in, see how that type of action produces certain patterns of responses to typical situations, and then formulate rules that describe these patterns. Then, evaluate the consequences of the rule rather than each individual act.

Thus, an individual action is justified if it is the kind of action required by a correct moral rule; and a moral rule is justified if it produces as much utility as alternative rules if everyone were to follow them. When I promise to repay the loan to my friend, I notice that I've made a promise, and that is a type of action covered by a rule such as 'When you make a promise, keep it'. Rather than evaluating the action by itself, I apply the principle of utility to the rule that governs the action. Since it can be plausibly argued that rules demanding that we keep our promises promote the general welfare and are thus required by the principle of utility, I can conclude that I should keep my promise to my rich friend and repay the money.

Notice the different results we get with rule utilitarianism. Act utilitarianism, remember, advocated in some cases that I not pay back the loan and give the money to charity. Rule utilitarianism, in advocating that we should follow rules directing us to keep promises, is closer to common sense morality. Rule utilitarianism produces similar common sense results with regard to the issue of justice and rights. Rules prohibiting slavery and protecting a range of individual rights insulate all of us from the tyranny that majorities can often impose on minority groups or individuals. Thus, rules guaranteeing individual rights promote the general welfare and are justified on utilitarian grounds. The rule utilitarian is arguing that the odd results that afflict act utilitarianism are the result of not taking the role of rules in moral reasoning seriously. Once we see morality as essentially a rule-governed activity, the implausible results of utilitarianism disappear.

However, rule utilitarianism has a fatal flaw. Anyone with much experience in life knows that sometimes we have to make exceptions to rules, especially because rules can come into conflict. Rules need some flexibility. But if the rule utilitarian adds flexibility by coming up with a rule such as 'Always keep your promises, unless it would produce bad consequences', then she is essentially reverting to act utilitarianism. Given the way the rule is constructed, the rule now specifies that we evaluate the act – act utilitarianism. The act utilitarian does not have to operate without rules; all she is committed to is the obligation to weigh the consequences of following a rule or not in particular cases. The fact that there is a rule prescribing the action does not matter – only the consequences matter. If the consequences of breaking a rule are negative then even the act utilitarian would say obey the rule. Thus with a rule constructed in this way there is no difference between rule and act utilitarianism.

To preserve the difference, the rule utilitarian must insist on strict rules with no exceptions, so that we are precluded from evaluating the particular case. However, if the consequences of breaking a rule are positive, the rule utilitarian must insist on following the rule despite the consequences, since the rule cannot admit exceptions. But, then, she is no longer a utilitarian because she is not appealing to consequences as a justification.

The point here is that even if it is usually a good thing that people follow rules, it is even better when people follow rules when they produce good consequences, but break them when they produce bad consequences. Thus, any utilitarian must be an act utilitarian, and that saddles utilitarianism with all the difficulties of act utilitarianism raised above.

There is no question that sometimes our reasoning is and should be focused on the consequences of our actions and their contribution to the general welfare. However, given the serious objections raised above, this fails as a comprehensive theory of moral reasoning.

KANTIAN DEONTOLOGY

We have seen how moral reasoning that focuses exclusively on consequences often sacrifices individuals in favour of the general welfare. By contrast, deontological theories assert that individual persons have a special status, and because of that status, we owe them respect that must not be violated regardless of consequences. On this view, respect for persons and their rights and duties are the building blocks of moral reasoning. This approach to morality received its most impressive formulation in the work of Immanuel Kant, who we encountered in Chapter 1.

In Chapter 1, we rejected Kant's account of autonomy. However, many contemporary advocates of deontology think the substance of Kant's account of moral reasoning can be defended without endorsing his peculiar view of freedom. According to Kant, persons have special status because they have intrinsic value. Something has intrinsic value if its goodness is part of its nature, independently of its relation to anything else. Persons, according to Kant, have intrinsic value because we are capable of making rational, independent judgements regarding how to live. (Remember, given the results of Chapter 1, that Kant is wrong to think that independent means independent of all causal influence, emotions, or desires.)

This capacity for autonomy (which remember, for Kant, involves both freedom and reason) makes us utterly different from any other entity. Artefacts and natural objects such as non-human animals, plants, etc., have value only if someone or something has a use for them. They have only extrinsic value because their value is dependent on their relation to something else that confers value on them. They are good not for their own sake, but for the sake of something else. This means that artefacts and natural objects can be the source only of what Kant calls hypothetical imperatives. Remember from Chapter 1 that a hypothetical imperative is a principle that commands us to do something only if we want to. For example, 'If you need to travel long distances, then buy a car.' A car has value only if people need to travel. 'If you are hungry, then eat that piece of fruit.' The fruit has value, only if someone finds it desirable.

Human beings have extrinsic value and can be the source of hypothetical imperatives. My mechanic has value because he can keep my car running smoothly. Regarding his ability as a mechanic, he is valuable only to the extent someone wants his services. However, in contrast to artefacts and non-human natural objects, human beings have intrinsic value in addition to extrinsic value. Human beings are not just mechanics or family members or enjoyable companions, useful for this purpose or that. Human beings have value, even if no one cares about them, even if they are of no use to anyone, even if their behaviour is despicable. Thus, they have what Kant calls objective worth and must be treated with special respect.

According to Kant, this fact about persons has substantial impact on our moral conduct because, once we recognize that human beings have objective worth, we cannot treat them *merely* as instruments to promote the common good or any other purpose. This means that moral reasoning must proceed, not from hypothetical imperatives, but from what Kant calls a categorical imperative.

A categorical imperative is a principle that commands us to do something independently of what we want. 'Categorical' means without conditions attached. A categorical imperative is one that I must act on under any conditions. What is the content of a categorical imperative? These considerations regarding the unconditional value of persons lead directly to one of Kant's three formulations of the categorical imperative. (We will be considering only two formulations here.) 'Act so that you treat humanity, whether in your own person or in that of another, never as a means only, but always at the same time as an end in itself.' (Kant, 1964, Ch. II, section 428.)

This means that we must respect the fact that other persons have ends (i.e. interests, goals, projects, etc.) and they are capable of reasoning about these ends and acting on those reasons. Thus, any treatment of another person must be supported by reasons to which that person would assent if she were thinking rationally.

If I ask my mechanic to repair my car, I am using him as an instrument. However, in paying him the amount agreed upon, I am treating him as an end in himself, as someone with his own interests and reasoning ability, and whose time is valuable. Assuming I am not coercing or deceiving him, I am treating him in a way to which he consents, and therefore my treatment is justified. If I were to run off without paying, then I would be using him as an instrument for my purposes without his consent. I would be treating him as having only extrinsic or conditional value, and that is forbidden.

Kant's theory is in sharp contrast to utilitarianism. The demand to treat all persons as ends, not merely as a means, will forbid the sacrifice of individuals for the sake of the common good. Kant's theory requires a variety of duties, to tell the truth, keep promises, be fair and just, etc., that we must follow independently of their consequences.

Kant was not interested only in explaining why we have an obligation to respect the humanity of others. He also wants to provide a systematic way of determining, in particular situations, when our actions are justified and when they are not. Thus, he provides an alternative formulation of the categorical imperative that helps in this task. 'Act as if the maxim of your action were to become by your will a universal law.' (Kant, 1964, Ch. II, section 421.) Kant claims that this formulation is equivalent to the earlier formulation. We will not worry here about whether that is the case. We will be concerned with the reasoning process generated by this principle.

Kant claims that when we think through what this principle means and apply it to situations that arise in life, we can determine whether an action is obligatory or forbidden. The maxim of your action is the principle to which you would appeal if someone asked you to justify your action. It describes from a subjective point of view the principle on which you act. For instance, suppose I have to write a term paper for my ethics class but never get around to writing it. So, I decide to buy a term paper off the Internet. My maxim would be 'When I am required to submit a term paper, and haven't written it, I will submit a paper I have purchased as my own.' But Kant, like Nagel, argues that as a rational being I must be consistent. Therefore, I have to treat my maxim as a general rule that applies to all similar cases. The maxim then becomes 'Whenever I need to submit a term paper, and haven't written it, I will purchase one and submit it as my own.' Notice that the categorical imperative says 'Act *as if* the maxim of your action were to become, *by your will*, a *universal law*.' The phrase 'as if' and the reference to a universal law directs me to imagine a hypothetical situation in which everyone follows this general maxim. The phrase 'by your will' asks me if I could consistently want this situation to come about.

Thus, I am to universalize my maxim. Can I consistently want all students to submit term papers they have purchased rather than written themselves? Any maxim that issues in a permissible action must be universalizable. Kant, of course, lived long before anyone could purchase papers over the Internet. But given Kant's discussion of how to handle similar cases, he would surely have said no. To want everyone to follow this principle would produce what he calls a contradiction in the will. The idea is that if everyone were to purchase a term paper, professors would stop assigning term papers and evaluate students using some other assignment. Thus, I would want to receive a grade by submitting plagiarized work, and also want to create conditions under which submitting plagiarized work would be impossible. I want contradictory situations to exist. Because the principle, if followed universally, would produce a contradiction, the principle is irrational. Because it is irrational, the action following from the principle would be wrong. I have a duty to refrain from submitting plagiarized work as my own.

Other maxims that advocate actions that are intuitively wrong suffer a similar fate. We must not steal since if everyone did so it would undermine the system of property that we want to take advantage of by stealing. We must not lie because, if everyone did that, it would undermine the system of communication that I seek to take advantage of by lying. We must not break promises because, if everyone did that, it would undermine the practice of making promises. We must not kill innocent persons because, if everyone did that, it would leave me open to being killed. The basic message here is similar to the golden rule – 'do unto others as you would have others do unto you' – though it differs in that the categorical imperative is allegedly based not on what I want but on what I can consistently will.

It is important to be clear that Kant is not appealing to consequences here. He is not saying that if I submit plagiarized work it will cause others to do the same, thus causing the system to collapse. That would be a utilitarian style of reasoning and Kant is opposed to that. He is not concerned with the actual consequences of our actions. He is concerned about whether the concept embodied in the principle is coherent or not. The imagined consequences are purely hypothetical and serve to highlight whether I am thinking clearly about what I am about to do. An action is wrong, not because it has bad consequences but because it is irrational in its conception. Thus, reason binds us to morality. Morality makes demands on us that are inescapable simply because we are rational. Immorality is opposed to reason.

From this formulation of the categorical imperative, Kant thinks we have a powerful decision procedure for determining what our duties are. If an action is forbidden by the categorical imperative, it allows no exceptions. It is wrong regardless of consequences. This aspect of Kant's theory might seem implausible on the face of it. It is natural to think that morality is about benefiting others – making life better for them, avoiding causing them harm, etc. What could be more beneficial than causing good things to happen? What is the source of Kant's complaint about consequences?

As we have seen, an exclusive focus on consequences tends to obscure the intrinsic value of persons that Kant takes very seriously. But he has other worries as well. Kant is sceptical that we can all agree on what counts as a good consequence. Human beings disagree about what counts as happiness or wellbeing. Each of us has our own conceptions of the good and Kant doubts that we can discover an objective account of happiness that would resolve this disagreement. Thus, we can make progress in moral philosophy only if questions of what is right or wrong take precedence over questions about what is good.

Furthermore, Kant is very concerned with the stability of morality. If what is right or wrong differs from person to person, culture to culture, or situation to situation, social life will lack the trust and intelligibility necessary for us to flourish. Focusing on consequences cannot provide this stability. The consequences of our actions are very hard to predict. We can seldom be certain about the long-term effects of our actions. Moreover, given that we cannot fully control the consequences of our actions, it is wrong to praise or blame people for them. We cannot be held responsible for them and thus they should not be part of our evaluation of an action.

Given these worries about instability and responsibility, we need to anchor morality in something that can be good in all circumstances without any qualifications. Kant thinks he has found that in what he calls 'the good will'. The good will is the only thing that is good without qualification. Anything else we might value – pleasure, happiness, intellect, courage, loyalty, etc. – can be put to evil purposes.

The only thing that cannot be used for evil is a good will – the intention to follow the moral law. The content of this good will, the law we must follow, is the categorical imperative.

This provides stability because the rightness or wrongness of actions is not affected by anything outside the stipulations of the categorical imperative. If an action is obligatory according to the categorical imperative, its moral worth is not affected by whether it achieves its goal or not – it is still obligatory. Even if the actual consequences are disastrous, the moral worth of the action is unchanged. Moreover, the moral worth of an action has nothing to do with the underlying emotions or desires that may have caused the action. If I tell the truth because I am worried about being caught in a lie, my action has no moral worth because it was motivated by fear. If I tell the truth because of compassion I feel towards the person who might be harmed by my lying, my action still has no moral worth. It was motivated by an emotion. The only proper moral motive is respect for the moral law. I am worthy of moral praise only if I act out of a sense of duty in recognizing what is rationally required.

Similarly, if an action is forbidden, its moral worth is unaffected by whether the agent intended to achieve some good with it, or whether she was acting courageously, intelligently or out of loyalty. The moral worth is wholly determined by whether the agent has a good will, and the quality of the will is wholly determined by whether the universalized form of the maxim produces a contradiction. Thus, luck cannot affect the moral worth of an action. Nothing outside the agent's control can affect the moral worth of an action since moral worth is wholly determined by the content of the will. You can be blamed only if your maxim is forbidden by the categorical imperative.

In summary, as persons we have to see ourselves as moral agents who have interests, who can rationally deliberate about those interests, and choose based on that deliberation. Once I see myself in this way, I must see others as possessing the same capacities. Thus, as a rational being, consistency requires that I take the objective worth of individuals seriously and that commits me to assessing actions according to the categorical imperative.

Kant's theory is brilliantly rendered and rests on some very plausible intuitions. Persons are worthy of respect and should never be used solely as a means to an end to which they do not consent; persons are responsible only for that which is in their control; and morality consists of principles that are in force for everyone at all times. It seems quite reasonable to adopt these elements of Kant's theory.

However, just as there are difficulties with utilitarianism, there are deep problems here. Some of the problems involve the internal mechanics of the theory. Kant gives us few guidelines on how we must construct our maxims, but the issue is crucial in determining whether an action is right or wrong. To illustrate, suppose someone asks me if I am going to take care of some important business I don't want to do, and to avoid embarrassment, I am considering lying about it. My maxim would be 'Lie when you don't want to reveal the truth.' As Kant says, this would not pass the categorical imperative test because if everyone were to do this, the practice of giving credence to the statements people make would break down. However, suppose I re-write my maxim as follows 'Lie when you don't want to reveal the truth, if you can do so without anyone finding out.' This would not violate the categorical imperative, since if everyone did this, there would still be good reason to believe most of the statements people make. It is usually unreasonable to think no one will discover our lies, so the situation will not arise very often. If everyone followed this maxim, our communicative practices would not be useless. Thus, this maxim would pass the categorical imperative even though it is intuitively wrong. Apparently, when we place conditions and restrictions on our maxims almost any action will pass the categorical imperative test. This would be way too permissive.

Given this result, it looks like we have to restrict maxims to very general ones such as 'Lie when you do not want to reveal the truth.' Given that this would fail the test, we would be morally required to always avoid lies. But that is an implausibly demanding moral requirement. Intuitively, sometimes telling the truth is the wrong thing to do, if it is going to seriously harm someone. Thus, it appears that when maxims are properly formulated they will produce very strict duties such as 'always tell truth', 'always keep promises', 'never kill innocent people', 'never take someone else's property without their consent', etc. Although these are fine as basic guidelines, clearly the complexities of life require exceptions to every rule. Kant's theory apparently produces an impossibly rigid morality.

Furthermore, Kant gives us no advice on how to deal with conflicting duties. The duty to tell the truth and the duty to keep promises can come into conflict. Conflicting loyalties, multiple promises that cannot all be kept, incompatible duties to help others are constant elements in our lives, and any viable theory of moral reasoning must tell us something about how to reason through them. But Kant's theory is mute on this.

Finally, Kant claims that keeping promises, respecting the property of others, etc., are necessary because if everyone were to violate them the very practices on which the violations depend would fall apart. But suppose someone had no interest in keeping promises or respecting property. Suppose someone does not care how he is treated, as long as he does not have to worry about treating others well. Such people would not feel the force of Kant's contradiction in the will, and thus such violations would not be wrong for them. The stability Kant was seeking disappears. Moreover, in such cases it appears that whether something counts as a duty or not depends on desires or interests, not reason alone.

Like utilitarianism, Kant fails to provide a comprehensive conception of moral reasoning that can be applied in practical contexts. To be fair, both of these theories, originally articulated in the eighteenth century, have received the attention of many generations of philosophers who have elaborated their details with increasing complexity. Contemporary versions are far more elaborate and sophisticated than I have had space to represent here. Yet, most of the problems mentioned above persist in some form or another and neither theory has achieved anything like a consensus. After 200 years, this ought to mean something. What has gone wrong?

OBJECTIVITY RECONSIDERED

Notice that both theories inspect the tangled web of desires, feelings, and the local, provisional, thoroughly practical reasons we use to justify our actions. Out of that web, they try to identity a single feature that stands out as basic, that provides the key to unlocking the patterns of thought that must organize this bloomin', buzzin' confusion (to use a phrase made famous by William James) into something eminently reasonable. For utilitarianism, it is the balance of good consequences over bad. For Kant, it is the dignity of our freedom and reason. But when we test these theories by reintroducing that tangled web of desires, feelings and practical reasons we are left with something that seems less attractive than the bloomin', buzzin' confusion with which we began.

The theories do not seem to answer the practical questions we ask when facing moral dilemmas, or they answer them in ways that seem utterly incompatible with life as we know it. We can trace the source of the problem to the demand that moral reasoning be objective. As moral agents, we confront the world as selves-in-relation, as individuals bound up in relationships, with limited knowledge, and substantial restrictions on emotional, cognitive and volitional resources. We look at matters from a distinct point of view that we come to through personal experience, a point of view that is deeply informed by the things in our lives that we care about. From this point of view, we develop our habits of thought and feeling. We also develop a conception of our projects, goals, a sense of how life should extend into the future. This personal point of view constitutes everything that is meaningful to us.

Any moral theory that strives for objectivity must implicitly advocate that, at least for the purposes of moral reasoning, we leave this perspective behind. Both utilitarianism and Kant demand that we adopt, at least temporarily, a perspective-free standpoint that allegedly enables us to survey reality from a God's eye view. But we cannot achieve this God's eye view. We are inevitably bound to the perspectives that we have; and thus all the messy details of life flow back into the picture to disrupt the neat system of logical distinctions and carefully calibrated principles.

We can and ought to stand back from our desires and interests and think about whether we want to be motivated by them, whether they are right for us and for others with whom we associate. However, while adopting this reflective stance and reasoning about what to do, our desires and interests are still very much ours. As philosopher Bernard Williams argues, merely by thinking about what to do, I am not transformed into a being whose interests are universal. In other words, I do not acquire the motivation for morality merely by thinking about this universal interest.

This raises the question why we would want to adopt this God's eye view given that everything meaningful is bound up in that perspective which the God's eye view enjoins us to leave behind. If I were somehow to leave behind my particular perspective, so I no longer have my interests and projects in mind, what would motivate me to do anything at all? Why would a person who cares about moral considerations and ordinarily acts on the basis of desires and interests that are related to her life in particular ways find it reasonable to deliberate from a point of view lacking those motivational resources?

In this chapter, we have been considering the question whether objective moral reasons have their own motivations independently of our desires and interests. It is difficult to see how such reasons could become a reason *for me*. This is why both utilitarianism and Kantianism have trouble explaining the motivations of morality. I began to address this problem for Kant in Chapter 1. In this chapter, we have more reason to suspect this approach to ethics.

In summary, according to Kant we are motivated to act simply out of respect for the moral law, what Kant calls 'the jewel within,' to which we are to respond with reverence. In essence, we are acting out of respect for our capacity to make universal laws. This may be inspiring, but it is hard to see why such reverence ought to replace the more concrete reasons we have for caring about our lives and the people we encounter.

Utilitarianism raises similar worries. When we trace the implications of applying the principle of utility to everyone affected by our actions, it is so demanding that it is incompatible with any reasonable account of human psychology. Remember that utilitarianism asks us to choose the course of action that produces the best overall consequences. Suppose that when you get home from work or school, you enjoy listening to music (or watching TV, playing with the kids, etc.). Is there something else you could do with your time that would advance the general welfare? Of course there is. You could work in a soup kitchen, solicit funds for famine relief, or work 16 hours a day and give all your money to charity. According to the principle of utility, you must choose one of them rather than your favourite activity since that would produce more aggregate wellbeing. We are always obligated to adopt the good of everyone else as our goal, independently of our own interests. Any time you pursue a personal project, even if you are being productive, you should be doing something that would have wider ramifications. Given our best current understanding of human psychology, this is unreasonable. Although human beings are diverse and some people may be able to live this way, most of us would find such a life lacks an important dimension of meaning.

Thus, it is a gross distortion of human nature to think that we can give up our separate projects and goals in favour of a desire to impartially promote the general welfare. Though we are capable of altruistic actions, it is impossible for us to have an equal concern for everyone all the time. At bottom, both utilitarianism and Kantianism fail to take into consideration how human beings care about the world, a topic we will explore in Chapter 5.

None of this suggests that these accounts of rational deliberation have not produced important results. The influence of utilitarianism and Kant on our moral reasoning has been substantial, and much good has come about because, for generations, people have taken these ideas seriously. The general welfare is one of our concerns but only one among many. Respect for our freedom and reason is important but no more so than the variety of other concerns that compete for our attention.

Note that even Nagel's modest account of objectivity cannot adequately explain our motivation for morality. Nagel is right that, as rational beings, when our beliefs or actions are inconsistent we have some motive to resolve the contradiction. But that motive competes with the variety of other motives that drive human behaviour and we are not given any reason why we must always seek to scratch that itch more than others. This is not to suggest that impartiality is not important in moral reasoning. As we will see in subsequent chapters, it is very important in certain contexts. However, the kind of impartiality human beings are capable of will not be the sort described here.

To briefly return to a theme from Chapter 1, notice that neither theory can explain Schindler's motive for rescuing his workers. Given Schindler's life of fluctuating fidelities and persistent self-aggrandizement, there is little evidence that he typically responded to worries about the general welfare or the 'shining jewel' of the moral law within. More plausibly, he grew to hate Nazis and developed bonds of affection towards his workers that he could not bring himself to sever. The way in which these moral considerations bear on a moral perspective will be considered in subsequent chapters.

The aim to develop morality into a system of logically related principles supported by the authority of an objective standpoint is a worthy goal, and the underlying motive for this pursuit I suspect is not peculiar to philosophers but is shared by most people. The motive is to achieve moral clarity, to be able to act with resolution, confidence and a clear conscience and to find some common ground on which all of us can stand. Moral theory tries to find clarity and common ground by demonstrating that logic forces morality upon us. Because all of us are at least potentially rational, logic creates a common, indisputable framework that we can all get behind despite our competing interests. Thus, if the authority of moral claims came from the objective point of view, it would allow us to follow that logic unencumbered by biases, perspectives or particular interests.

Non-philosophers are more likely to look for clarity in a religious perspective resting on the certainty of faith or in adherence to the traditional principles that have guided a community or society, and appear stable because they have withstood the test of time. It is unclear how common ground or genuine certainty emerges from these resources. It may be the case that morality simply is not an area of human practice that can ever achieve the kind of clarity and certainty we seek, and we will have to live with something much more contingent and ambiguous.

Our analysis of the objective stance towards morality has highlighted a variety of important moral considerations that must be part of our reasoning about morality. They include the common good, the basic equality of human beings, consistency and reciprocity in reasoning, the moral worth of individuals, our self-understanding as autonomous persons, the importance of rights, etc. Our philosophical tradition has highlighted these considerations and has explained their importance – this is no small accomplishment. Yet, our analysis does not reveal a compelling system that links these considerations together. It does not demonstrate that there are natural priorities that determine their relative importance. We are left with a variety of competing claims, competing considerations and seemingly many different ways of using them in our everyday judgements.

This returns us to the issue of pluralism. A variety of competing and sometimes incompatible claims is just what pluralism asserts. Neither utilitarianism nor Kant have given us reason to reject pluralism. Where does that leave the goal of moral clarity and the search for common ground? Does value pluralism leave us with a stark choice between tolerance for views we find offensive or the use of force to resolve conflict, given the limitations of our reasoning capacities? The answer to this question is no, although further analysis is necessary before we can support this claim. However, clarity and common ground are unlikely to emerge from an inquiry that breaks apart our perspectives and tries to reconstruct them as a God would see them. Rather clarity and common ground must emerge from within the form of life that we live, a topic we will explore in the next chapter.

REFERENCES AND SUGGESTIONS FOR FURTHER READING

Benedict, Ruth (1934), *Patterns of Culture*, New York: Penguin.

Bentham, Jeremy (1988) [1789], *The Principles of Morals and Legislation*, Buffalo, NY: Prometheus.

Brink, David O. (1989), *Moral Realism and the Foundations of Ethics*, Cambridge: Cambridge University Press.

Harmon, Gilbert (1975), 'Moral relativism defended', *Philosophical Review*. 84, 3–22.

Kant, Immanuel (1964) [1785], *Groundwork of the Metaphysics of Morals*, trans. H.J. Paton, New York: Harper and Row.

Krausz, Michael (ed.) (1989), *Relativism: Interpretation and Confrontation*, Notre Dame: Notre Dame University Press.

Levy, Neil (2002), *Moral Relativism: A Short Introduction*, Oxford: Oneworld Publications.

Mill, John Stuart (1969) [1863], *Utilitarianism*, ed. J.M. Robson, Toronto: University of Toronto Press.

Nagel, Thomas (1987), 'The Objective basis of morality', in *What Does It All Mean?*, New York: Oxford University Press, 59–75.

Rosenstand, Nina (2003), *The Moral of the Story* (4th ed), New York: McGraw-Hill.

Smart, J.J.C. and Williams, Bernard (1973), *Utilitarianism: For and Against*, Cambridge: Cambridge University Press.

Williams, Bernard (1985), *Ethics and the Limits of Philosophy*, Cambridge: Harvard University Press.

CHAPTER 3

MORAL REASONS IN CONTEXT

Chapter 2 concludes that objectivity is not an adequate foundation for moral reasoning. If objectivity cannot ground our moral reasoning, what can? In this current chapter, I want to explore the possibility that the foundation for moral reasoning lies in our relationships. We discover what morality requires of us and make judgements about what sort of person to be, and justify our actions through our capacity to reason within the context of the various relationships that make up our lives. But what kind of relationships? After all, exploitation and oppression characterize some relationships. Surely, these are not the appropriate foundation for moral reasoning.

The kinds of relationships that offer the most plausible rationale for ethical concerns are caring relationships. This is because, by caring for people as well as objects, ideas, institutions, etc., we express through our actions what has value for us. And ethics seems inextricably bound up with value.

This brings us to a new theory that has recently received a good deal of attention called the ethics of care. Although this is a relatively recent theory, it has historical antecedents, especially in the work of the eighteenth-century British philosopher David Hume. However, we will not explore Hume's philosophy but will begin with contemporary versions of the theory. The ethics of care takes caring relationships such as that of parent, friend, medical practitioner, teacher, etc., as the paradigm for how we ought to treat others generally. Relationships in which one person must care for another or in which there is mutual care are the crucible in which we develop moral capacities. Thus, moral reasoning is a process of deliberation and appropriate feeling developing out of our capacity to care. In part, the purpose of moral reasoning is to sustain the caring relationships that are central to our lives. This means that caring relationships take precedence over other concerns, since they are the basis of an ethical life. Unlike the other theories we have discussed, for the ethics of care, emotions are central to our capacity to reason effectively.

AN ETHICS OF CARE VS. AN ETHIC OF JUSTICE

Though the ethics of care is a philosophical position, it first emerged in psychology because of work on the development of moral reasoning skills in children. In the late 1960s, the moral psychologist Lawrence Kohlberg published research that seemed to show that children's moral development occurs in six stages that roughly correspond to the development of other intellectual skills. As very young children, we do as we are told to avoid punishment. We soon recognize that if we do things for others, others will help us, which is the second stage of moral development. In the third, adolescent, stage, we begin to seek approval from others and thus conform to prevailing norms. Later in adolescence, we gain respect for law and authority and learn that others respect us for being honourable and law-abiding. As young adults, we adopt a conception of autonomy and the idea that social life is a contract whereby individuals can do as they please as long as they do not harm others. Some individuals finally achieve the highest stage of moral reasoning, a Kantian perspective in which we are no longer ruled by self-interest, the opinion of others or fear of punishment but live according to self-imposed universal principles such as those of justice and respect for the dignity of persons.

This understanding of moral development was challenged by Carol Gilligan, a member of Kohlberg's research team, who noticed something peculiar about Kohlberg's data. Kohlberg's early research focused on boys. When he later included girls in his sample, they seldom reached the highest stages of moral development, tending to reach only the stage of seeking approval from others. Kohlberg concluded that girls do not have a clear sense of justice or the logical capacity to arrive at moral conclusions. After reviewing Kohlberg's data and conducting her own reasearch, Gilligan concluded that Kohlberg had misinterpreted the data. She argued that girls' moral reasoning is not inferior to boys. Instead, they tend to reason differently about moral issues. For example, in one of Kohlberg's interviews he asks two 11 year olds, Jake and Amy, the following question: Should Heinz steal medicine from a pharmacist in order to save the life of his sick wife if the pharmacist refuses to lower the price so Heinz can afford it? Jake said Heinz should steal the medicine, and used as a justification the principle that life is worth more than money. But Amy hesitated to draw a clear conclusion. She said that it was wrong for Heinz to steal the money but also wrong for the pharmacist to refuse to help Heinz acquire the medicine. She worried that if Heinz was caught and had to go to jail, then there would be no one to take care of his wife. She finally said that if we could talk to the pharmacist perhaps he would agree to donate the medicine.

Kohlberg thought Amy's hesitation to articulate a clear answer showed that Amy does not understand the concept of justice, and that she has not yet learned how to apply an abstract concept to a particular case in order to arrive at a conclusion. But Gilligan argues that Amy is viewing the situation differently from Jake. Amy does not see this case as a question of abstract rights in conflict – the wife's right to life vs. the pharmacist's right to sell his property as he wishes. Rather, Amy sees the situation as one in which each individual participates in a variety of relationships on which they depend. The solution to the dilemma involves preserving these relationships. Amy is concerned about Heinz's wife, but also the possibility that by stealing the medicine, Heinz may end up harming his ability to care for her. She is also hopeful that the pharmacist may in the end be a compassionate person who may resolve the dilemma by responding with the appropriate emotion.

As Gilligan points out, feelings of care direct Amy's reasoning. Because Kohlberg's model of moral development did not fully acknowledge the importance of this style of reasoning, he interpreted it as a deficient form of moral reasoning. Gilligan's research, of course, is not dependent on a single case. She has interviewed many girls and women over the years and these interviews show that certain themes dominate women's thinking about ethics. When moral conflicts arise, women seek to preserve the relationship. Thus, feelings of empathy and compassion, a willingness to listen, a reluctance to control others, and a recognition of the fragility of relationships, play an important role in reasoning. Although women recognize the importance of moral rules, they decline to rigidly adhere to them if doing so might cause harm.

Gilligan's conclusion is that boys and men tend to focus on an ethic of justice being primarily concerned with applying moral rules that specify rights and duties, an approach that draws from everyday versions of the deontological and utilitarian theories described above. Girls and women tend to focus on appropriate responses to particular individuals in concrete relationships – what Gilligan calls an ethic of care.

Though Gilligan claims to have traced broad tendencies within populations, she notes that this distinction between an ethic of care and an ethic of justice is not absolute. Boys have a tendency to focus on rights and duties, but there are many exceptions. Generalizations about girls are similarly qualified by exceptions. The implication is that the theories of morality discussed above and the dominant ways of reflecting on morality in Western society are persuasive only because of the traditional male dominance that has characterized our culture. Given the traditional roles that women have occupied as mothers, nurses and teachers, caring has played a more central role in the lives of women than in the lives of men and this accounts for the different approaches to moral reasoning that Gilligan identifies.

Gilligan's research is still controversial, as is Kohlberg's, and this is not the place to evaluate these psychological studies. However, the philosophical issue we will explore is whether the ethics of care provides an intelligible account of moral reasoning, one that promises to improve on deontological and utilitarian views.

Utilitarianism and deontology are philosophical representations of what Gilligan is calling an ethic of justice. By 'ethic of justice,' Gilligan means a moral perspective that relies on a system of rules that agents are required to apply to particular situations in order to guarantee fair and equal treatment. In this system of rules, the features of persons that matter are features that everyone shares – our ethical concerns arise because people exhibit the general features of personhood. For Kant, those general features have to do with our human capacity for freedom and reason. For utilitarians, we are morally concerned for others because all human beings (and many non-humans as well) can suffer and have interests that can be harmed. The features that make an individual unique are not relevant. We are to treat everyone with equal respect and concern regardless of our particular relationship with them or the peculiarities of their personality. As a result, as I discussed in the previous chapter, reasoning within an ethic of justice proceeds impartially, striving to be as objective as possible. Given these parameters, an ethic of justice is primarily concerned with the protection of individual rights in the Kantian case, or improving the general welfare in the case of utilitarianism.

By contrast, the ethic of care takes our responsibilities within relationships as the most important moral considerations. Thus, ethical issues are framed as issues that arise within particular relationships and can be dealt with only as a participant in a relationship. Because we are in relationships not with persons having only the abstract, general features of personhood, but with particular persons with their unique, individual features, we must focus on the particularity of persons and their unique situation as members of relationships. This means that our reasoning cannot be impartial because it must place special emphasis on our deepest involvements in which we have a special interest. People with whom we have a caring relationship have priority.

We have to be careful to precisely locate the difference between these two positions. One might think that the difference lies in what the object of moral concern is. That is, the ethic of justice is more concerned with making sure we conform to correct rules that protect rights and specify obligations that hold for all persons, while the ethic of care is concerned with the welfare of individuals with whom we are in immediate contact. But this would not be the right way of understanding the contrast between the two positions. An ethic of care is also concerned to protect rights and impose obligations, and an ethic of justice (especially the utilitarian version) is concerned with promoting the welfare of the individuals affected by our actions. The difference is not in the object of concern but in how we are to frame moral issues and reason about them.

For an ethic of justice, we derive the justification for how we should treat someone from an impartial moral principle – the categorical imperative or the principle of utility. And that principle plays such an important role because it is responsive to features that all of us, as persons, share. According to Kant, all persons are worthy of equal respect and concern because we are free, rational agents. For the utilitarian, all human beings are worthy of equal respect and concern because we all have interests that can be harmed. We derive the universal moral principle from universal generalizations about human beings, and from that universal principle, we derive specific moral rules that we must apply to particular circumstances. We often refer to this as top-down reasoning because it begins with universal generalizations, which we then apply to particular cases.

By contrast, for an ethic of care, we justify actions by appeal to the dynamic of the relationships of the particular people involved, and we solve problems by working within the relationship, not by impartial, disengaged judgement. For instance, although you may be able to make some rough generalizations about how you should treat a friend who has acquired a nasty drug habit, these generalizations are not going to be subtle enough to guide you in dealing well with the situation. Each friendship will require its own response tailored to the person about whom you care.

In a friendship, you care about the particular person, not because she is a human being but because she is a particular, unique person. You don't consider her interest equal to the interests of others, but are partial to her interests – that is part of what it means to be a friend. We often refer to this reasoning as bottom-up reasoning, because it begins with an understanding of particular cases and arrives at a conclusion using primarily information about that particular case. So we frame issues in terms of which general principles are in play in an ethic of justice. We frame issues in terms of what is important in a particular context (especially a relationship) in the ethics of care.

To avoid misunderstanding, it is important to emphasize that neither Kantianism nor utilitarianism denies the importance of intimate relationships for human flourishing. Both can grant that we have reason to favour our friends or family members in many situations. The contrast with an ethic of care is in the underlying rationale for ethical conduct within such relationships. For utilitarianism and Kant, the ethical treatment of friends and family members must be derived from an impartial principle. By contrast, proponents of the ethics of care will argue that conduct that exhibits ethical care is not derived from more basic principles but is itself basic.

This disagreement about what is basic vs. what is derivative marks a fundamental division between these two approaches to moral reasoning. According to proponents of the ethics of care, when we make impartiality the fundamental aim of our moral reasoning we will have a tendency to alienate ourselves from the very people to whom moral concern is supposed to connect us. In striving for impartiality, we need not see others as the individuals they are but rather as familiar examples of human beings in general. We have the leeway to disengage from relationships that matter the most to us, because the ways of caring essential to these kinds of relationships are not moral requirements. Instead, moral experience is dominated by obligations to generalized others or to abstractions such as the general welfare or the moral law.

Thus, given our limitations in time and energy, we are discouraged from treating the people we are closest to with the partiality they deserve. Conflicts inevitably arise between obligations to family and friends vs. obligations to more distantly related people, and in striving for impartiality we avoid favouring familiar others. Disengagement becomes a habit, and morality becomes a barrier to human relationships rather than an aid. This disengagement is not mandated by an ethic of justice. Rather, it is the natural by-product of organizing our moral lives around the need for impartiality. The more we strive to be impartial, the less attention we pay to our deepest involvements and commitments.

Furthermore, according to proponents of the ethics of care, because the details of situations in which moral judgement is crucial are often unique and unrepeatable, we cannot rely on general principles to the extent both Kantians and utilitarians advocate. For example, top-down reasoning has little to say about the degree of responsibility one should assume to help a friend with an addiction, because we must tailor the answer to that question to the circumstances.

Of course, there is another side of this debate. For proponents of traditional theories such as Kant or utilitarianism, when we treat different people differently and allow our biases and preferences to enter the picture we risk injustice and unfairness. Moral failure is all too often the result of taking care of those close to us while failing to pay attention to those with whom we have no personal connection. Moral corruption is usually a product of making ourselves and the things we care about an exception to which moral rules do not apply. Furthermore, without principles to guide us from the top down, our judgements are likely to differ so much from situation to situation that morality would have no stability. Kant's worries about stability are indeed real concerns.

Who is correct? Must reasoning be top-down and strive for impartiality, though we can never quite attain it as we saw in Chapter 2. Or should moral reasoning be bottom-up, firmly situated in particular contexts and relationships. To sort out this question, we should first entertain the possibility that these contrasting positions are too starkly drawn. There may be a middle position we can adopt.

DOES MORAL REASONING REQUIRE MORAL PRINCIPLES?

There is no doubt that the ethics of care places greater emphasis on context and particularity than has traditionally been the case in moral philosophy. However, there is substantial controversy even between advocates of a care ethic over the role that moral principles should play in our reasoning. Some philosophers who think that care should play a central role in our moral lives nevertheless argue that the activity of caring can best be understood as a way of maximizing utility (utilitarianism) or demonstrating respect (Kantianism). Thus, they will argue that, while the ethics of care has pointed to areas of human activity often ignored by traditional moral discourse, the activities of caring are grounded in the concepts generated by Kantian or utilitarian theories. For these theorists, the ethics of care is new wine poured from old skins, an insightful, new way of elaborating the traditional theoretical positions. In other words, when you care about someone, you want the best for them and treat them with respect, and this is essentially what Kant and the utilitarians were advocating in their distinctly different ways.

However, care involves elements that make it distinctly different from traditional theoretical perspectives. First, you can respect a person and never treat her merely as a means to your ends, even though you care nothing about what happens to her. As long as your conduct does not harm her, you can be indifferent to her fate. However, if you care about someone, their fate matters to you independently of whether your actions have an effect on them or not. Second, although it may be the case that when I care for my daughter I am advancing the general welfare, thus doing exactly what the utilitarian wants me to do, in many cases I could be doing something else that does even more to advance the general welfare. Thus, there is real conflict between participating in caring relationships and advancing the common good. Third, many of our actions in close relationships might fall under a general principle such as 'protect your family from harm', or 'help your friends when they are in need'. However, to do any of these things effectively, you need care in addition to acting on a principle. In order to protect your family from harm or care for friends you need to do more than follow rules – you have to have the right emotions, recognize and respond to their unique needs, etc. Thus, the care perspective is not simply another way of talking about the common good or respect for persons. It is not a simple matter to assimilate the ethics of care to a utilitarian or deontological model.

Philosophers who think that the ethics of care is a unique perspective tend to argue that the ethics of care entails moral particularism, a relatively recent development in philosophical accounts of moral reasoning. Moral particularism is the view that the rightness or wrongness of an action is wholly determined by the context or situation in which the action occurs. Thus, to determine if an action is right, we have to look at the situation itself and the various factors that are relevant to morality in that situation rather than appealing to rules or principles. Is it wrong to tell a lie? According to the particularist, we cannot answer that question without attending to the particular situation in which the lie occurs. In many contexts, lying is wrong, but in other contexts, it may be the best thing to do, and we cannot determine this by applying a general principle.

Where is the evidence that we need principles in order to act well? Apparently, we do not always need to rely on principles. If a pilot ditches her damaged plane in a small warehouse in order to avoid a high-rise apartment building, knowing that a few workers in the warehouse will be killed, most people would say she did the right thing – she sacrificed few to save many. But the very same people would likely say that it would be wrong to harvest the organs of a few healthy warehouse workers without their consent in order to save the lives of many ill apartment dwellers, even though such an act would sacrifice a few to save many. Most people, at least those who have not taken a philosophy class, would not be able to immediately point to the principle at work that enables them to distinguish these cases. They can make an appropriate judgement without a principle.

Nevertheless, given sufficient opportunity to think about matters, most people would recognize that a medical system that allows the harvesting of organs from healthy people would have a variety of drawbacks and would be able to come up with a principle to cover cases like this. Thus, a defender of moral principles might say that although people do not always formulate a principle to act on, they can if they need to justify their actions. Thus, although principles need not be part of the decision-making process that leads people to act, it is important that principles justify our actions.

But this is precisely what the particularist denies. According to the particularist, the principle is a way of organizing our thinking about cases after the fact. It is not something we require to make justifiable decisions – we are able to distinguish the pilot's case from the organ harvesting case without the principle, which we cook up later to describe decisions made by using our understanding of a situation. What matters is that we can distinguish an emergency (the aeroplane crash) from an institutional practice (if organs were routinely harvested). We are able to distinguish between these contexts, not because we have a principle to help, but because we are good at marking similarities and differences between contexts.

Moral particularism appears at first glance to be a radical position. Not only are the abstract principles of Kant and the utilitarians largely irrelevant. Even ordinary principles such as the golden rule or 'thou shalt not kill' fail to provide reasons for our actions. In fact, at first glance, moral particularism seems to be incompatible with the ethics of care. Proponents of the ethics of care are often interpreted as holding the position that when justice and care come into conflict, care should always override justice. Our obligations that derive from the actual relationships we have with family, friends, etc., should always take precedence over abstract moral concerns like that of justice or rights. Proponents of the ethics of care are apparently implicitly adopting a general principle such as 'always seek to preserve your close relationships'.

However, this criticism misunderstands both the ethics of care and moral particularism. To explain what I mean, we first have to clarify what moral particularism asserts and what the reasons are for holding such a position.

Particularists argue that contextual judgement is required even before we know what principle might justify an action. Recall from our discussion of Kant in the previous chapter that the first task in applying the categorical imperative is coming up with a description of one's action in order to determine whether the principle applies or not. This step caused considerable problems for Kantian-type theories because of difficulties in deciding how general or specific a maxim must be. The moral particularist argues that there are no rules for how we should describe our actions. Thus, contextual reasoning is required even before we can formulate a rule on which to act.

Think of the various act descriptions that might figure in a moral principle – lying or truth telling, cruelty, kindness, theft, murder, rape, respect, etc. Although we can often use these words without controversy to accurately describe our actions, it is not because we are implicitly following a rule. What rule can we use to determine whether a speech act counts as a lie? We might formulate a rule that says, 'If an action is a false assertion intended to mislead it is a lie.' But we routinely make false assertions intended to mislead that do not count as lies. When someone asks, 'How are you?' I often respond by saying 'fine' when I am not feeling well at all. In most contexts in which such statements arise, I should not be accused of dishonesty. We intentionally deceive children about all sorts of things, tell jokes that intentionally mislead, and recount tall tales, but we do not classify these as lies either. To exclude those cases that should not count as lies, we might include in our principle that a lie must intend to harm the person being deceived. However, false statements made under duress are often not lies though they may intend harm to the person deceived. Moreover, lies are usually intended to protect the liar rather than to harm the person deceived, so if we include this in our principle we will exclude lots of cases that we routinely call lies. It is not obvious we can construct a principle about what counts as a lie that captures the messy details of ordinary life.

Let's try a different example. What rule do we use to identify acts of cruelty? We might formulate a principle that any action that results from an intention to inflict physical or psychological pain is cruel. But coaches, parents, teachers and opponents in competitive sports, among many others, inflict pain in routine circumstances – marathon runners inflict it on themselves. But these usually don't qualify as examples of cruelty. We might add that for an act to be cruel the victim of the action must be in a relatively powerless position, which would exclude reasonably fair athletic contests from consideration. But, as any parent knows, powerless people can often be cruel to the more powerful; so being in a relatively powerless position is not a necessary condition.

We might then add that the pain must be excessive or unnecessary to qualify as cruel, but judging that something is excessive or not does not look like a rule-guided decision. Determining what counts as excessive is very much context dependent differing from situation to situation. This is just the point of the particularist critique of the use of rules – all the work of classifying actions is done by our judgements about what is important in a particular context. The principles are at best summaries of how we have described clear cases of lying or cruelty in the past. However, each situation we encounter is unique in some way or other, and because these unique features of situations can significantly affect our judgement about how to classify our actions, the rule by itself cannot justify a classification. In other words, after collecting all the clear cases and formulating them in a principle we still have a further question to ask – Is there something in the circumstances of the immediate situation that makes the typical classification suspect? The point is not that we cannot decide how to classify actions – we are usually quite good at it. The point is that the classification does not follow logically from a rule, but rather emerges from our skill at understanding the significance of the various features that a situation presents.

Furthermore, according to the particularist, the problem with rules and principles does not end once we settle on an act description – a similar problem arises when we try to apply principles. Suppose we accurately describe an assertion as a promise. Consider a simple principle such as 'Always keep your promises'. A moment's reflection would show that no reasonable person would endorse such a principle.

Suppose I make an immoral promise – in a fit of rage I promise to kill a colleague of mine because of a disagreement we have over school policy. Obviously, I am not obligated to keep that promise and the principle would not be sufficient justification for such an action. But this doesn't show there is a problem with moral principles, only that the principle is too simple. Principles that can cope with the complexity of human existence must allow for exceptions. So let's reformulate the principle – 'Always keep your promises, unless you have made an immoral promise.' But once again, there are obvious exceptions to such a principle. If I have promised a friend that I would attend a concert in which he is performing, and at the last minute, an ill family member calls needing transportation to the hospital, I am under no obligation to keep the promise. So let's reformulate the principle again. 'Always keep your promises, unless you have made an immoral promise, or the promise is overridden by a more important obligation.' But what counts as a sufficiently important overriding obligation? Obviously, preventing harm to a family member is more important than my attendance at a concert. But suppose the performer at the concert is a close friend who is giving her final concert capping an illustrious career, and the ill family member often feigns helplessness in order to get attention, and has a variety of other reliable transportation options. In this case, my obligation is not so clear.

Notice that in such a circumstance, to know what one should do requires attention to the property of the situation that stands out as the most important one to act on. Is it the fact that the performance is given by a long-term friend, or the fact that it is a final, capstone performance, or that a family member is making the request for assistance, or is it the fact that in your best judgement, the family member is being manipulative? The moral particularist argues that there is no principle that will guide one's judgement here. What matters is not the fact that you made a promise but the content of the promise when balanced against competing considerations. The only way to make a decision here is to assess the competing features of the context and determine *in this case* which is most important. Generalizations about other cases involving promise-keeping will be of limited help because other cases are unlikely to be like this one – involving this particular friend, at this point in his career, and this particular family member with her unique characteristics.

The defender of moral principles has a response to this argument. She will grant that there is no principle that will make a final decision for us – any application of a principle in complex circumstances requires judgement. We have obligations to friends and family members, obligations to show appreciation and gratitude and to prevent harm when possible. Which obligation is most important here is a matter of judgement. However, principles play an important role because they tell us what our obligations are, or to put the point differently, they tell us which considerations are always relevant regardless of context.

In the case under discussion, I may not have an actual obligation to fulfil the promise I made to attend the concert, but the fact that I made a promise is always a central consideration. On this view, our judgements must be responsive to moral principles, although often they cannot be derived from them. W.D. Ross developed such a theory that was designed to enable principles to co-exist with contextual judgement. Ross argued that morality consists of a variety of principles that we know intuitively. We ought to tell the truth, keep promises, make reparations for wrongs we have committed, seek the distribution of happiness in accordance with merit, do good for others, do good for ourselves, and avoid harming others. He calls these *prima facie* duties because they tell us what to do as long as there are no overriding obligations. However, because there are usually conflicting obligations, we can determine our actual duty only by situational judgement, not by a principle.

The problem with Ross is that on his view the only thing that can override an obligation is another obligation. I can violate my promise to attend the concert only if I have another competing obligation. But suppose I find out before leaving for the concert that my friend of many years has been spreading scurrilous rumours about me. I no longer feel like honouring her career. It seems unreasonable to claim that I am still under this obligation to keep my promise under these circumstances. Yet, there is no competing obligation here, only a change in what I feel like doing. There are countless circumstances in which it is reasonable to fail to keep a promise simply because one's preferences or desires have changed. In fact, it is fair to say that the list of exceptions to a rule that one must always keep promises is infinitely large – in principle not something that can be captured in a finite principle. The particularist is not arguing that we can never justify keeping promises. Rather, the point is that the justification is not based on a principle but is based on a highly developed skill at understanding what is significant in particular cases.

In the philosophical literature on this debate between principle-based reasoning and particularism, there is much controversy concerning how best to characterize moral particularism. Some particularists take the extreme position that moral principles do not exist and play no role in our reasoning. But that seems false. As I noted above, principles are best understood as summaries of our collective experience – they are generalizations that capture what is typically advocated within our moral institutions given what we know about how they function. We know that dishonesty usually gets us into trouble, and that promise breaking undermines relationships and can destroy the fabric of trust on which society depends. In order for a person to have good moral character, he or she must have lots of this kind of understanding. Just as reasoning in any other domain requires information and an understanding of basic concepts, moral reasoning requires a wealth of background generalizations on what is typically the case, generalizations that can be summarized by a principle.

Moral principles situate us in a framework of considerations that usually have special weight if we are to reason well. When an action involves the infliction of pain on someone who is relatively powerless, the possibility of cruelty should take centre stage in our reasoning; acts of deception should always provoke worries about undermining public trust and the dignity of the person being deceived. Moral principles and rules that govern act descriptions are reminders that place these considerations at the centre of our thinking. Moral particularists need not deny any of this. However, moral particularists should argue that principles and their application are never sufficient to justify an action; they play an important though limited role in moral reasoning.

Ultimately, principles play a limited role in moral reasoning because of the complexity and instability of the contexts we confront. Especially in modern societies with increasingly complex interactions that are subject to constant change, each of us confronts situations with a variety of dimensions that must be considered. It is a highly regarded cautionary principle of reasoning in science that the more dimensions that are introduced by a hypothesis the riskier our generalizations are, because it is likely that new dimensions will introduce features that influence the significance of the original data the hypothesis is designed to explain. This is even more appropriate in the moral realm because moral properties do not have the fixed characteristics of properties studied in physics and chemistry. In short, we risk making mistakes in morality if we rely too heavily on moral principles because they, by their very nature, encourage us to focus on the shared features of situations rather than each situation's unique characteristics.

Given this account of moral particularism, we are in a better position to understand the kind of reasoning encouraged by the ethics of care and required by pluralism. Recall that I said one of the problems with the ethic of care is that it seems to relegate considerations such as justice to a secondary status, since we are to give priority to caring relationships and that might entail treating others unfairly.

Given our understanding of moral particularism, considerations of justice need not play a secondary role in an ethics of care. When we look at the contexts in which we make moral decisions, most of them involve relationships, and we make fewer moral mistakes if we attend to the details of those relationships when reasoning about moral questions. Like the other theories we have investigated, the ethics of care provides directives about where to look for the most salient moral properties – a way of flagging moral features that we often overlook. The ethics of care is flagging the bonds of care as the features of a context that should receive our attention.

In some cases, impartiality and a concern for justice is just what we need to make the right decision. In fact, it is hard to imagine how our caring relationships could function without a sense of justice. Parents must treat their children fairly and must sometimes be impartial. All caregivers must make difficult decisions about how to distribute their care and this inevitably leads to concerns about justice. For example, a nurse recognizing that a terminally ill patient is in extraordinary, untreatable pain may want to respond to a patient's request to help her die. But to do so may violate a professional duty to do no harm. Care giving routinely involves such difficult conflicts between personal responsiveness and recognition of duties.

The ethics of care need not advocate that we never act impartially or out of a sense of duty. Rather, we should never act impartially or out of a sense of duty without due attention to those features of our circumstances that an impartial principle would fail to identify as relevant. The concern for impartiality, justice and duty emerges out of the relationship and its particulars, not in spite of these contextual features. Relationships place demands on us that are not demands of this particular relationship only but are demands that arise from the type of relationship it is. Appropriate standards of care are determined not only by the particularities of this nurse and this patient but also by general features of the nurse-patient relationship. The requirements of parenthood, in general, play some role in determining what counts as being a good parent.

Thus, an ethic of care cannot ignore or subordinate considerations of justice, fairness and impartiality. In many cases, they must be front and centre. The difference between a care ethic and other moral theories is not that an ethic of care minimizes the importance of justice and impartiality. Instead, an ethic of care views justice and impartiality within the context of relationships.

THE ROLE OF EMOTION

When we view moral reasoning from the perspective of moral particularism, we can better understand another unique aspect of the ethics of care – the prominent role of emotion. According to the dominant traditions in moral philosophy, including the utilitarian and Kantian views, in order to acquire moral wisdom we must step back from our desires, emotions and sentiments because they interfere with objectivity. On this view, human beings tend to focus too narrowly on their self-interest. The purpose of moral reasoning is to correct this tendency. However, emotions and desires, since they are immediate expressions of our subjective states, only encourage this unfortunate tendency to be self-centred. Although emotions may be essential to moral response once we have decided what to do, the process of deciding should not be encumbered with feelings that will cloud our judgements, according to traditional theory.

By contrast, the ethics of care argues that emotions and desires are essential to achieving moral wisdom. Although feelings sometimes distort our reasoning, they need not do so. Moreover, emotions and desires are crucial for understanding what morality requires – moral reasoning cannot be effective without them.

The role of emotions in moral reasoning is related to the discussion of act descriptions and moral particularism above. Regardless of the theory of moral reasoning one holds, we cannot begin to reason about a particular case without being aware of the morally relevant features of a situation. However, as noted above, the details of the social circumstances in which we must make moral decisions are complex and subtle. Just as human beings have a disturbing tendency to emphasize our self-interest, we have an equally disturbing tendency to ignore what is right in front of us. How often do we fail to perceive the fact that a friend is in despair or one's spouse is feeling ignored? We pay attention to crime when it is committed in white neighbourhoods, but ignore it when the victims are black. We know that hunger and poverty exist in our neighbourhoods but do little to correct the problem. The most natural explanation of these moral failures is that we are not sufficiently concerned – attentiveness is a function of what we care about.

To say that one cares about someone is in part to say that one's psychological state is primed to notice what that person needs and to respond to those needs; and emotional connection with the person cared for is an important component of that psychological state. Parents are more likely than other adults to notice the needs of their children, and friends are more likely than strangers to pay attention to each other's wellbeing, because these relationships are characterized by genuine bonds of affection. Doctors and nurses are more likely to perform their jobs effectively when they care enough about the patient's interest to feel some degree of empathy and compassion. Just as a heightened state of fear helps one to pick out dangers in the environment, a heightened state of empathy or compassion engages our capacity to notice morally relevant properties.

Furthermore, it is important that our care not be merely a concern to be a good parent or good doctor, or even to care about justice or ethics. Though it is important to care about such things, our ultimate concern must be for the individual people who are the recipients of our care. As the moral particularist points out, moral situations deal with concrete individuals who have specific histories, identities, feelings and ways of looking at the world that are often unique, novel and incapable of being expressed in generalizations. To do the right thing in these circumstances requires that we attend to these particularities. This suggests that we must be careful not to rely too much on stereotypes and broad generalizations when reasoning about moral questions, because if we do we will tend to see others not as they are but as we construct them.

As much as possible, moral conduct requires that we see the world as others see it. All human beings are connected to reality via various feeling states, and therefore if we are to understand others we must understand their feelings as well. And this requires that we not strive for emotional distance, but rather emotional connectedness.

Thus far, I have described the role of emotion in moral reasoning as an aid to helping us notice things about others that might otherwise go unnoticed – what we might call attentional focus. But moral reasoning is not simply a matter of attending to the appropriate properties, but involves properly conceptualizing our situation as well. There is a difference between seeing that someone has intentionally made a false statement and acknowledging that they have told a vicious lie, between seeing someone as hungry and acknowledging the injustice in her hunger. In order to distinguish between rough sex and rape we have to understand the intricacies of consent, a complex concept. In other words, moral reasoning is not just a matter of perceiving a new detail in a situation but of understanding the moral relevance of what we see.

This dimension of moral reasoning also involves emotion because displaying the appropriate emotional response is a necessary condition for having the appropriate moral concept. Suppose for instance that I witness an insurance salesperson selling an unnecessary but expensive insurance policy to an elderly women suffering from senility. It is one thing to recognize this as morally wrong, quite another to be outraged by it. To simply note the moral wrongness without experiencing moral indignation is a failure of understanding, a failure to understand the moral importance of the act. To note that an action is one of extraordinary charity but fail to admire it is to miss something about the action. The other moral emotions of disgust, guilt, regret, remorse, shame, etc., function similarly. They provide us with understanding regarding the social world in which we participate.

Care belongs on this list of moral emotions. When a friend is suffering, the person who acts to relieve that suffering solely out of a sense of duty without experiencing appropriate emotions such as worry is failing to grasp the significance of suffering. In summary, a person who lacked the capacity for moral emotion could not grasp the full significance of moral actions. Emotions enable us to grasp features of a situation that are otherwise inaccessible.

These considerations regarding the importance of particularism and the emotions refer us back to the discussion of agency in Chapter 1. In Chapter 1 we rejected the idea that we can achieve autonomy by separating ourselves from others. In this chapter, we find reason to reject the idea that the more abstract and impartial our moral knowledge is, the better it grasps reality. Instead, the more connected we are to others and the more concrete and context sensitive our understanding is, the better our actions are able to conform to the shape of reality.

PROBLEMS TO SOLVE

Moral particularism and the ethics of care solve some of the difficulties with utilitarian and Kantian accounts of moral reasoning discussed in Chapter 2. Unlike utilitarianism, the ethics of care focuses on the unique, particular aspects of persons and thus takes distinctions between persons seriously. It does not permit sacrificing individuals for the common good. Like utilitarianism, but unlike Kant, the ethics of care gives us a handle on how to deal with some conflicts between moral requirements. We are permitted to be partial towards those we care about – emotional connections, degree of understanding, etc., permit us weigh some considerations more highly than others. However, unlike utilitarianism and Kant, the ethics of care does not seek a standardized decision procedure for ethics and thus need not worry about quantifying happiness or constructing universalizable maxims. But more importantly, by rejecting a central role for objectivity, the ethics of care provides us with a framework for understanding moral questions that is compatible with the important role that personal projects and relationships play in our lives. Since large portions of our lives are devoted to relationships of some sort, the ethics of care is rooted in concrete experience rather than abstract entities such as the common good or the moral law. As a theory, it is more intuitive and natural than deontology or utilitarianism. Rather than demanding the sacrifice of what is most meaningful in life, it welcomes those attachments and views morality as an organic product of those attachments.

However, the ethics of care and moral particularism pose problems of their own. Some issues we must address are internal to the theory itself. How do we determine the relative strength of moral properties in a particular context? As I noted above, this often has to do with experiencing the proper emotion. But how can we be reasonably sure that our emotions are appropriate without reintroducing the dispassionate reason that earlier theories endorsed? What standards of correctness are involved? We should view ethical problems as problems within relationships that we can solve only through mutual dialogue and agreement. So does any product of this mutual dialogue and agreement count as a correct answer to the problem? The answer has to be no. Obviously, there are good agreements and bad ones. There are solutions to problems that allow people to flourish and solutions that only create more trouble. Thus, we must have some standard beyond what people work out through their relationships. But this seems to lead us right back to traditional theory in which we seek an impartial perspective from which to assess these agreements.

Although the ethics of care resolves conflicting obligations by permitting us to place more weight on the needs of those with whom we have a caring relationship, does the ethics of care provide us with any understanding of what to do when relationships of roughly equal value conflict?

Furthermore, the ethics of care advocates that we do what we can to preserve relationships – the right thing to do is often that action which has the best chance of preserving the relationship. But many relationships are unhealthy and should be terminated. Thus, an ethic of care must provide some standard for assessing relationships.

In addition to these worries about the internal mechanisms of the theory, we have to address external criticisms regarding a care ethic's ability to make sense of our lives. Perhaps the most glaring difficulty is that, as I have characterized it thus far, the theory supplies no guidelines for how we ought to treat strangers or those with whom we have no relationship. One of the virtues of theories that ground morality in objectivity is that they are universal theories – all moral agents are due equal respect and concern. Though we might quibble with how they explain this notion of equal respect, the fact that both utilitarianism and Kantian theories take our common humanity seriously is an important advantage in their favour. Unless the ethic of care can supply an adequate account of this idea of our common humanity it will not measure up.

In this connection, we must say more about how an ethic of care, especially when connected to moral particularism, protects the reasoning process from succumbing to biases and prejudices. What is to prevent sexism, racism and other forms of discrimination from entering the picture if we assign greater importance to those with whom we are familiar? I suggested above that impartiality and fairness are an important component of many relationships. But what about treatment of those with whom I have no relationship?

In addition, we must address the problem of instability. Some philosophers argue that it is better to act out of a general moral principle like 'help those in need' than a particular caring feeling like compassion, because principles don't come and go like emotions do. Intuitively, if I am obligated to do something, the force of the obligation is independent of how I happen to feel today. If we allow emotions to influence our judgements, our judgements will change from day to day (or minute to minute) as our emotions fluctuate. How can we rely on moral judgements that are so unstable?

Finally, we must revisit the issue of whether our theory of morality describes a plausible way of life. The ethics of care enables us to place substantial weight in our moral deliberations on the elements of life that we find most meaningful, especially relationships. As I noted above, this makes the theory intuitive and natural, in keeping with how most of us live. But the theory is intuitive and natural only if it can clarify when it is permissible to refuse to care for others. If the burdens of care are too great then the theory is so demanding that it suffers from the same problems as utilitarianism and deontology – it requires us to sacrifice the very things that make life meaningful. A super abundance of care may be no more attractive than a life of impartial disengagement. It may be just as demanding as utilitarianism.

To whom are we to devote our caring resources and how should we distribute these resources? Are we to care only for those we are familiar with, those who are part of our network of relationships, those who are fellow members of a religion, ethnic group or profession, those we like? As I noted above, this would seem to introduce the possibility of all kinds of bias and prejudices. Or, are we to care for everyone indiscriminately, including those who are reprehensible, disgusting or contemptible? This would require that we give up our own projects in just the way utilitarianism demands. Clearly, the notion of care must be elaborated in more detail. Subsequent chapters are designed to provide solutions to these difficulties.

The ethics of care makes use of our actual motives and abilities. But it can succeed only if we can conceptualize a moral relationship with a wider range of beings than the familiar others on which the ethics of care focuses. We will now turn to the concept of obligation, which will help us understand the role our common humanity plays in moral deliberation.

REFERENCES AND SUGGESTIONS FOR FURTHER READING

Card, Claudia (ed.) (1991), *Feminist Ethics*, Lawrence Kans.: University Press of Kansas.

Gilligan, Carol (1982), *In A Different Voice: Psychological Theory and Women's Development*, Cambridge: Harvard University Press.

Hooker, Brad and Little, Margaret (eds.) (2000), *Moral Particularism*, New York: Oxford.

Kohlberg, Lawrence (1971), 'From is to ought: How to commit the naturalistic fallacy and get away with it in the study of moral development', in T. Mischel (ed.), *Cognitive Development and Epistemology*, New York: Academic Press.

Noddings, Nels (1984), *Caring: A Feminine Approach to Ethics and Moral Education*, Berkeley: University of California Press.

Nussbaum, Martha (1986), *The Fragility of Goodness*, Cambridge: Cambridge University Press.

Nussbaum, Martha (1990), *Love's Knowledge: Essays on Philosophy and Literature*, Oxford: Oxford University Press.

Ross, W.D. (1930), *The Right and the Good*, Oxford: Oxford University Press.

Walker, Margaret (1998), *Moral Understandings: A Feminist Study in Ethics*, New York: Routledge.

CHAPTER 4

OBLIGATION

We have encountered the concept of obligation already, especially in connection with Kant's theory. However, we have not said much about what an obligation is and what sort of work it must do. By looking closely at the idea of obligation, we can begin to make sense of the idea that morality makes demands on us.

A moral obligation or duty is a moral requirement that directs an individual to do or not do something. We typically express obligations in statements that contain the word 'should' or 'ought', but the moral sense of these words has an additional authority associated with them. We often use the words 'should' or 'ought' to mean that we should do something or bad consequences will follow. 'I should go to bed at 11:00 if I want to be alert tomorrow.' But I am not morally obligated to go to bed at 11:00. By contrast, the moral use of 'should' or 'ought' often, though not always, expresses the thought that we are morally required or forbidden to perform a particular action – that an action is obligatory.

Our moral world is amply populated with obligations. When I make a promise, I have an obligation to keep it. I have obligations to my students, friends, family members, credit card companies, a duty to vote, an obligation to refrain from harming other persons, to respect other persons, to show gratitude when receiving a favour, obligations to animals and other natural objects, I probably should never destroy a work of art, etc. To be obligated is a common human experience. Yet, despite the pervasiveness of obligations, they do not exhaust our moral categories. Many actions are morally good but not obligatory or morally bad but not forbidden – it might be a morally praiseworthy act should I decide to give all of my salary to charity, but I am not obligated to do so. It might be a moral failing if I am usually short-tempered with associates, but I am not forbidden to be that way. Nevertheless, we can express an important part of morality as a duty or obligation.

The philosophical problem is to understand what obligations are, to identify their source, determine what is owed and to whom, and to give an account of what justifies obligations. Of course it might be the case that our common sense idea of obligation is mistaken or unintelligible, in which case the philosophical task will be to suggest how we might reform our concept.

In connection with this task of understanding, obligations have two features that any adequate theory of obligation must explain or make intelligible. The first is that obligations are very difficult to escape. Once you have one, it is yours whether you want it or not. A parent has an obligation to care for her child even if she no longer wants children. I have an obligation to pay for my car even though, after driving it for 10,000 miles, I wish I had made a different purchase. Another way to put this point is that obligations bind our will – they restrict what we morally can or cannot do regardless of our desires. In ordinary discourse, we refer to this inescapability as a product of the conscience.

There are some restrictions on this inescapability. Most philosophers think that 'ought implies can'. That is, we must carry out obligations only if we are able to do so. If I promise to deliver a lecture in New York and all flights into the city are cancelled due to bad weather, I am no longer obligated to perform that action. And an obligation can be overridden by a more important obligation. Thus, a theory of obligation must give guidance on how we assess the relative importance of obligations when they come into conflict. Keeping in mind these restrictions, an obligation is among the strongest reasons we have for doing or not doing something. Thus, in ordinary discourse we often say that a person must or must not act when she is under an obligation – the proposed action is a moral necessity.

This inescapability is in part what is philosophically puzzling about obligations. When a person says, 'I must keep this promise,' what exactly does she mean by the word 'must'? A person making this statement is suggesting that keeping the promise is necessary. What kind of necessity is involved? Obviously, there is no physical necessity involved. A person who feels they must keep a promise is physically capable of not doing so. Many philosophers have argued that there is a kind of logical necessity involved with such a statement. Once one sees what the facts are and how reason must function, reason demonstrates that one and only one course of action is available – to keep the promise. The action is logically necessary.

A third possibility for what 'necessity' means in a moral context is psychological necessity. By 'psychological necessity' I mean that from the standpoint of my integrity as a moral being – the deepest commitments that make me who I am – I must keep the promise. The necessity arises because, if I am forced to act against my deepest commitments, I lose a sense of who I am. I can no longer identify with and therefore feel alienated from my actions. In ordinary discourse, we say 'if I did that I could no longer live with myself'. As we explore the concept of obligation, we will have to determine which account of necessity (or inescapability) is appropriate in moral contexts.

The second feature that a theory of obligation must explain is related to this inescapability. If something binds our will so securely, it would seem that there must be some authority behind it. To have authority is to have a legitimate right to command obedience. What commands our obedience when it comes to morality? This is a troubling question because obligations differ from other commands such as those of a military officer. It is often not clear who or what is issuing a moral command.

A theory of obligation must explain these peculiar features of obligation or provide compelling reasons to think we are mistaken about them. One way of explaining the authority that obligations have is by attributing their existence to God. Since God is owed obedience, at least within the monotheistic traditions, obligations that are the product of God's commandments would have the necessary authority to direct our actions. However, as I argued in the Introduction, it will not do to make morality thoroughly dependent on God. The authority of obligations must be established in some other way.

Traditionally, philosophers have taken two basic approaches to understanding obligations. Either obligations are grounded in facts about human nature, especially reason; or obligations arise from an implicit contract that exists among human beings. We have already encountered, in Chapter 2, the most widely accepted versions of the first option – deontological and utilitarian theories.

For utilitarianism and for Kant, moral authority lies in the objective foundations that define moral reasoning. Utilitarianism treats everyone's interests equally, thus claiming an objective basis for moral reasoning. According to Kant, moral principles must be universalizable, thus excluding particular interests from consideration. Authority comes from the position of being an impartial judge. Both theories identify a legitimate source of moral commands – the objective point of view.

How do they explain the inescapability of obligation – how do obligations bind the will? Because authority rests on objectivity, and objectivity is alleged to be a requirement of reason, both theories understand moral necessity in terms of logical necessity. However, given the difficulties that we have encountered in earlier chapters in establishing the intelligibility of the objective point of view, it is difficult to see how moral requirements are logically necessary. Although, arguably, from an objective standpoint, certain actions are required, the objective standpoint itself is not logically required. The questions raised at the end of Chapter 2 are relevant here. Why must moral agents see themselves as generating principles from a God's eye view? When we experience the pangs of moral conscience, is it because we are responding to the rational demand that we resist inconsistency in our reasoning? As argued in Chapter 2, reason is unlikely to supply, by itself, such a powerful motive. Thus, logical necessity does not adequately explain the phenomenon of moral necessity as human beings experience it.

What about psychological necessity? Can utilitarianism or Kantian theories explain moral necessity in psychological terms? Because act utilitarianism argues that what is obligatory depends solely on the consequences of our actions, which can change from circumstance to circumstance, the factors that bind the will, that constrain our desires and motives, must also change from circumstance to circumstance. This suggests that I should not develop strong motives to consistently choose a course of action. To put the point differently, what our conscience tells us to do must change depending on consequences. Thus, no *type* of action is morally necessary. For example, suppose I borrow a large sum of money from a wealthy friend, promising to repay it within a year. According to common sense morality, I ought to feel strongly about my promise to repay – the demand to repay is a moral requirement that is inescapable. But act utilitarianism suggests that if I can do more good by giving the money to charity, I ought to do so. Thus, my strong feeling of obligation to my friend is a hindrance to doing what I ought to do. It seems to follow, therefore, that I ought not develop strong inclinations to keep promises or repay debts. However, this is incompatible with a central feature of obligations – their inescapability.

British philosopher Bernard Williams has an especially poignant way of putting this point. Williams tells the story of George, who has a Ph.D. in chemistry but is having trouble finding work because poor health limits his job opportunities. George is eventually offered a well-paying job in a laboratory doing work on biological and chemical warfare. However, George has long been a committed pacifist, and his pacifism is central to his self-conception – it is part of what makes George who he is. In other words, pacifism is what Williams calls an identity-conferring commitment. If George takes the job he can probably slow down the development of these weapons or at least make sure they are less lethal. If George does not take the job, it will probably go to someone who is not a pacifist and will pursue the development of these weapons enthusiastically. Should George take the job? The act utilitarian would say yes. George would be helping his family as well as advancing the common good by limiting the development of dangerous weapons despite his unhappiness in the job. But Williams' point is that if George accepts the job, he will be forced to abandon who he is – his integrity is at stake. The deep commitments that sustain psychological necessity would be abandoned. Utilitarianism treats even something as central to personhood as identity as simply one source of utility among others. For Williams, the fact that certain beliefs make us who we are enables us to act with genuine commitment – there are things we must or must not do. A moral theory that advocates that we ignore such commitments cannot explain why or how moral conduct is possible, let alone necessary.

Let's see if Kantian deontology fares any better at explaining psychological necessity. Whereas utilitarianism devalues obligations and their connection to personal integrity, Kant's theory places obligation at the centre of experience. Recall that Kant argued that in order for us to make sense out of our lives we must assume we are free. We guarantee our freedom by rationally assessing our actions, submitting them to the judgement of the categorical imperative to make sure that desires, emotions, attachments or other commitments are not influencing us. I have a duty to act in accordance with the categorical imperative because only by doing so can I preserve my freedom and thereby preserve my personhood. Obligations are inescapable because in honouring them I preserve my freedom, which is essential to personhood.

The problem here is that Kant is wrong about the kind of freedom that is essential to our personhood. As I noted in Chapter 1, according to Kant, we are free only when we are free of causal influences. Among those causal influences are the attachments and commitments that result from our individual projects and conceptions of happiness. These commitments are what Williams referred to as identity-conferring commitments. I doubt that we can adequately conceptualize freedom and autonomy without some reference to higher-order desires, goals and purposes. Freedom is important to us because we care about whether we are free enough to realize our personal projects and our conceptions of happiness. Thus, the kind of freedom that is essential to personhood is the freedom to act in accordance with our deepest values, not the freedom to set those values and deep commitments aside in order to make impartial judgements. Without deeply held attachments and commitments, there is nothing for me to be – no identity conferring commitments that I must honour. If psychological necessity is explained by identity-conferring commitments, and Kant's conception of obligation is incompatible with such commitments, then Kant's theory cannot explain the moral necessity of obligation in terms of psychological necessity. Thus, Kantian theory is no better off than utilitarianism in explaining the nature of obligation.

SOCIAL CONTRACT THEORY

There is a long tradition in philosophy that rejects any attempt to ground morality in facts about human nature or human reason because we cannot seem to agree about which facts are the most important. This tradition is called contractualism or social contract theory, and it views moral obligations as products of agreements that human beings make.

Contemporary theorists have developed sophisticated contract theories that rely on Kant's most important insight, while rejecting much of the rest of Kant's theory. The central element of Kant's theory of obligation is that persons are ends in themselves. We should never treat a person solely as a means to some purpose that we might have. This means that it is appropriate to treat a person only in ways to which they would consent. The reason for this is that, according to Kant, no rational being could ever agree to have her reason subverted because that would be a contradiction in the will. Contemporary contract theory adopts this insight to develop an alternative conception of at least some moral obligations.

The idea is that agreements between people are justified if the agreements are freely arrived at. Thus, moral principles are not grounded in facts about human nature or reason. They are based on the fact that people have agreed to them – a contract. What is right is determined by what people can agree is right. Of course there is not and never has been such a contract in place to which everyone has agreed. However, that is not a problem according to the contract theorist because we can develop a theory about what sort of agreement to which it would be rational to agree – a hypothetical contract, not an actual one.

The most influential contemporary contract theory was developed by John Rawls in 1971. Rawls was concerned to develop a theory of justice, so his view applies only to the question of what principles should govern the basic political structure of society. But contract theories have been developed to justify a full range of moral concepts. Rawls sets out the task of trying to determine what kind of social contract everyone could agree to given the vast differences that exist between our conceptions of how to live. He asks us to imagine we are in what he calls the 'original position'. We are negotiators trying to decide what principles should govern the basic structure of society. In order to get agreement, we would have to imagine negotiators making decisions from behind a device called the 'veil of ignorance'. This means that the parties to the agreement cannot know whether they are rich or poor, male or female, intelligent or not too bright. In other words, they know nothing about their social status since such knowledge would introduce coercion into the agreement. Yet, they still know how to deliberate and know basic facts about human needs and how these needs are to be satisfied. The veil of ignorance is designed to show what agreements we can arrive at if no one is coerced and conditions of fairness obtain. Rawls argues that people under the veil of ignorance would consent to the 'greatest liberty principle' – a co-operative arrangement should involve the equal distribution of liberty, compatible with a like liberty for all. Because no one knows her social or economic status, each person would agree to equal shares of liberty for everyone because no one would want to take a chance of being deprived of liberty if they end up occupying a position of diminished social power. If you do not know whether you are a member of a minority group, you will advocate equal liberties. Otherwise, you run the risk of having your liberties curtailed. Liberties would include freedom of speech, freedom of religion, freedom of assembly, etc., – in short, the right to pursue one's own view of happiness.

Rawls also argues that the parties to the agreement would choose what he calls the 'difference principle'. For the same reason that participants choose the equal distribution of liberties, they will also choose roughly equal shares of economic goods as well. Everyone wants to avoid being disadvantaged and the only way to do this is to opt for equal shares. But because providing equal shares of economic goods may be inefficient, since some people are more productive than others and will only produce more if they receive compensation, some inequalities are necessary. However, any inequalities in wealth will be justified only if those inequalities are to the advantage of the worst off in society. Some people can earn more than others can only if that inequality helps those who are the least advantaged.

Most contract theories view obligations as derivable from rights. Thus, Rawls' theory justifies principles that define certain rights that people have – a right to equal liberties and particular claims on society's wealth. Members of society then have an obligation to honour this arrangement since it is what they would have chosen in the original position. Contract theories are appealing because they seem to clarify the source of moral authority. The basic idea supporting the moral authority of a contract theory is that an obligation is binding on me only if I have given my consent. The moral authority of the obligation is in my choosing it. It binds my will because I have given my consent to the agreement – I commit a deliberate, intentional act and thus cannot complain about the fact that I am now obligated. In effect, I have bound myself though the agreement. Thus, a contract shows respect for individual choice, as Kant's theory did, but the binding force of the agreement does not depend on a conception of reason that is divorced from the goods people are inclined to choose. Furthermore, the agreement creates conditions that others rely on. Other signees to an agreement have expectations that you will perform as specified in the contract. In signing a contract, you have encouraged others to rely on you, and the fact that you have created such an expectation binds you to uphold the agreement.

One difficulty is that, although contract theories clearly identify the source of moral authority, the sense in which obligations are morally necessary is less clear. Real contracts are easy to escape if one is willing to pay the consequences. Just as with contracts in business, there are costs to opting out of a social contract. Moral agreements are advantageous to individuals and opting out of the agreement would mean forgoing the benefits of the contract, and suffering social sanctions of various sorts. But signees to the agreement are free to do so, if they are willing to suffer the consequences. This suggests that moral agreements are binding only if you want them to be. As I suggested at the beginning of this chapter, obligations are binding independently of at least first-order desires. This suggests that a contract theory by itself could not explain all aspects of moral obligation.

Another difficulty is that some obligations are binding even though I did not choose them. Friendship involves certain obligations, though it is not a contract or promise (although in some sense it is chosen). In friendship, the intimacy of the relationship grounds obligations. Family relationships involve obligations but we do not choose these either. Thus, it is doubtful that contract theories explain the full range of obligations. This is not a worry for Rawls who restricts his theory to considerations of justice.

However, there is a deeper problem with contract theories such as that of Rawls. Rawls' contract is a hypothetical contract. No actual agreement takes place. But this means that the advantageous features of a contract discussed above are not doing any work in specifying the moral authority of contracts. Moral authority arises out of having actually agreed to something that others rely on. But no one actually agrees to or relies on hypothetical agreements. Thus, hypothetical contracts cannot trade on the moral authority of real contracts. Rawls' theory describes a contract that rational people would agree to under certain conditions. Thus, in such theories what does the work of justification is not the intentions of the agent or the reliance they create through their agreement. Rather it is the theory of rationality and the hypothetical choice situation that produces the moral requirements. Rawls is essentially arguing that under conditions of strict impartiality, where agents know nothing of their particular interests or circumstances, agents would care most about their liberty and would also be risk averse and choose principles that guarantee that the worst off members of society are not disadvantaged by the basic structure of society.

The problem is that we are right back to grounding obligations in facts about human reason, about which there is a good deal of disagreement. Since Rawls published his work, there has been much debate about what agents would choose in the original position. Many philosophers have argued that some people might be willing to gamble with their freedom or with their economic security in order to achieve greater wealth or opportunity.

But more importantly, we are right back to the problems we addressed earlier with demanding that reasoning about morality be objective. Rawls is arguing that we can get agreement on moral principles only if we reason under ideal circumstances – if we come to the table without our particular desires or interests. But none of us will ever reason in a context where our desires and interests play no role. Thus, even if Rawls is right about what we would choose, how much moral authority does such an idealization have? If someone is confronted by a real life situation in which her desires and interests are at stake, why would it be rational for her to limit her desires based on a hypothetical situation in which these very desires are not at issue? A hypothetical agreement cannot have the authority of an actual agreement.

One might argue that a theory that demonstrates what our obligations are under ideal circumstances is attempting to describe an ideal that we should strive to achieve. We may never be in a position where our desires and interests do not matter, but our reasoning should try to approximate such a situation as much as possible. But why should our reasoning in real life try to approximate reasoning in ideal circumstances?

This problem of understanding the moral force of hypothetical contracts is an instance of a difficulty that afflicts all of these theories of obligation we have looked at thus far. They all demand that when we reason about moral questions we do so from an impartial or objective point of view and that we invest this objective point of view with moral authority – an action is obligatory if it is justified from this point of view. But it is not obvious that we can make sense of this from a practical point of view, as a perspective that should guide our actions.

RELATIONSHIP OBLIGATIONS

What then does explain the moral authority of obligations and their inescapability? The ethics of care helps to answer this question. The ethics of care views our close, personal relationships in which one person is caring for another as paradigms through which we can understand moral obligation in general. What binds us in these relationships so that we feel obligated are the natural bonds that exist between parents and children, caregivers and patients, friends, etc. Obligation is thus rooted in feelings of connectedness with people about whom we care. Feelings of care and the deepening sense of relationship that occurs among intimates give rise to the thought that certain actions are morally required or forbidden.

These moral considerations have moral authority – a legitimate right to command obedience – because the maintenance of our relationships depends on them. They are inescapable because the relationships are deeply woven within our way of life and evoke extensive caring responses, and compromising them would produce considerable psychological pain. These claims are intuitively plausible. We keep promises to loved ones because, if we did not, the trust on which these relationships depends would unravel. Promises regarding important matters are inescapable demands because to show disregard for the expectations of someone you care about is cruel, and the emotional and cognitive states that support caring responses preclude excessive cruelty. That is to say, if you genuinely care about someone, you cannot intentionally cause her excessive harm while still maintaining feelings of care. This is a matter of degree. Unfortunately, we sometimes harm those we love. But if the harm is too extensive, at some point it is no longer plausible to say that feelings of care persist.

As we discovered in Chapter 3, objectivity within an ethic of care is derived from the requirements of certain relationships. We understand impartiality as a reflective ability to assess desires and commitments without thoroughly detaching ourselves from them. Thus, an ethic of care solves many of the problems with motivation that confront utilitarianism and Kant. It also provides plausible accounts of the two main features of obligations – the source of moral authority and the meaning of moral necessity (inescapability).

However, the problem with the ethics of care as a general account of obligations is that it tends to focus narrowly on intimate relationships.

However, we have obligations to persons with whom we are not intimate, and may have obligations to non-persons as well. How does the ethics of care account for these obligations? The strength of utilitarian, Kantian and social contract theories is that they give us a way of conceptualizing the intuition that all human beings are worthy of equal respect and concern. Historically, proponents and supporters of these theories have done much to promote the expansion of human rights. Extensions of these theories have been used to justify environmental and animal rights as well. If there is such a thing as moral progress in history, the expansion of human rights and the centrality of concerns about social justice that have occurred over the past 300 years qualifies as an example. Despite the theoretical flaws, there is much to admire in the ideas generated by Kant and the utilitarians. If the ethics of care is to provide a comprehensive understanding of moral obligation, it must make room for the intuition that we have obligations to all human beings and perhaps some non-human beings as well.

Despite the influence of the intuition that all human beings are of equal worth, we are apparently inconsistent with regard to this intuition. If people in our allegedly egalitarian, democratic society are asked 'are all human beings worthy of respect simply because they are human,' I suspect most people would say yes. If they were asked 'is any one person inherently of greater worth than another,' I suspect that most people would say no. Our moral ideals include the notion of equality. However, in practice we are not so egalitarian. The utilitarian Peter Singer uses the following two examples to point out our inconsistencies.

In his first example, Pond, a toddler falls into a pond and is in danger of drowning. All we have to do to save the toddler is wade into the water and retrieve the child. In his second example, Overseas, starving children need our money in order to purchase food and an appeal has been made for our charity. All we need to do is to send a cheque. Sending a cheque is no more difficult than wading into a pool. Yet, most people would say that in Pond we are morally obligated to retrieve the child, while in Overseas, there is no obligation. We can send the cheque if we want but it is not morally required. Singer, because he is a utilitarian, claims that we are inconsistent. What difference does distance make here when the harm is the same? To make matters worse, the dilemma is not between saving nearby lives instead of distant ones. The dilemma is between spending money for luxuries that we can use to save distant lives. Although ideally we think the moral worth of the child in Overseas is equivalent to that of the child in Pond, in practice we do not seem to hold to that ideal. Our perspective is partial to our own children, our neighbour's children, to our own goals and projects.

Singer and other proponents of utilitarianism, Kantian views, or social contract theory advocate that we reject partialism, because it is inconsistent with the idea that all human beings have equal moral worth. They argue that our intuitive attitudes are a moral failing that we can correct only by adopting an objective, impartial perspective. However, we have seen that given the way our lives matter to us, we cannot reject partialism and adopt impartialism. Yet, we have to make some room for the thought that we have obligations to strangers or people to whom we are not intimately related.

British philosopher Soran Reader suggests an explanation of our intuitions in the case of Pond and Overseas, which shows that arbitrary facts such as geographical distance are not relevant. Furthermore, Reader's explanation shows that our moral concerns need not be restricted to those to whom we are intimately related. Reader suggests that we understand 'relationship' to mean any relation that involves an actual connection between an agent and something else. An 'actual connection' is one in which there is some sort of contact or presence between the two things that are related, something that holds this connection together, and this connection must be of a sort that can be known by the agent. For instance, families are related through biological interaction or the institution of marriage, and this connection is reinforced through interacting within a way of life or through participating in common interests. We are related through history to people and environments that have shaped us and that we have shaped. We are connected through practical activity to the people and things we work and play with as well as the institutions in which this activity takes place. Environments connect people because of the need to share and distribute resources. According to Reader, these are genuine relationships because there is an actual connection between the people who constitute the relationship. Actual connection is, therefore, the source of obligations, and any relationship constituted by an actual connection can be the source of an obligation.

It is important to note that simply sharing properties is not enough to establish a relationship. All human beings as well as most animals share the capacity to experience pain, as the utilitarian suggests. But on Reader's view, that fact does not establish a relationship among all sentient beings and thus does not impose obligations on us towards all sentient beings. Only interaction or actual contact can establish a relationship and thus an obligation. Thus, living in the same neighbourhood, being of the same race, believing in the same ideology, or sharing a skill do not constitute relationships. But participating in block parties, joining a club, working for a political candidate, or working together in the office do constitute relationships.

Note also that the range of things that can impose obligations on us is extensive – not only friends and family but anything related through interaction, from a pet to an old baseball mitt. Of course, the content of the obligation will differ depending on the nature of the relationship. I have a different sort of obligation to my child than I do to a treasured artefact because the relationship is different. I will have more to say about the content of obligations shortly.

This approach to obligation helps to resolve one of the main difficulties with the ethics of care – the inability to account for the intuition that we have obligations to strangers. A chance encounter with another person is sufficient to establish a relationship that imposes an obligation. In a chance encounter, a person is present to me. She activates my senses. I register a variety of facts about her and begin to interpret her behaviour. She does the same with me. We become mutually aware of each other's subjectivity and I begin to think about her thinking of me, and her thinking of me thinking of her. Thus, questions about status and judgement come into play. Most importantly, there is potential for further engagement, so questions of vulnerability and control, hope and fear leap to the foreground of attention. In other words, an encounter, even with a stranger, activates a comprehensive way of comporting oneself. Any time lives are intertwined through an actual connection, a specific kind of relationship is constituted which creates specific obligations to which we must attend. None of this richly textured scene erupts with a person I have never encountered, regardless of how many characteristics we share.

Contrast the richness of an encounter with the connections between, for instance, myself, and Jane Wayne who lives in New Jersey. Jane and I have lots in common – we live in the same country, speak the same language, vote regularly, share a culture, participate in many of the same activities, perhaps read many of the same books, listen to similar music, etc. But we have never met and do not know each other. According to Reader, there is no relationship between Jane and me despite the fact we have much in common. The similarities and differences between us are of no consequence. I have no obligations to Jane because there is no relationship. Of course, if I were to encounter Jane, then obligations would arise.

This account of relationship obligations explains the different responses in the cases of Overseas and Pond. The encounter with Pond, a drowning child, creates an obligation to rescue because the encounter establishes a relationship. It is not obvious that a solicitation for famine relief in Africa is rich enough in real connections to sustain an obligation. How much of a relationship is there between wealthy inhabitants of Western society and starving children overseas? We see children in desperate need on TV or in other media where charity is solicited, and they may provoke feelings of empathy or compassion, which constitutes a kind of simulated relationship. But the connection is a weak one. According to Reader, this explains why, if we have an obligation at all, it is a minimal obligation.

It is important to be clear on the limits of this argument. I am not suggesting that we should ignore the fate of starving children elsewhere in the world. We should be more attentive to their fate, though not because we are obligated. Obligations are only one component in our moral world. They establish a minimal level of acceptable treatment of others, but do not exhaust the ways in which it would be good to treat others. We can fulfil all our obligations and still not be a very good person. People in need, such as in the case of Overseas, warrant our generosity because it is a good thing to be generous and we can be criticized for not being generous enough. But in the case of Overseas, what we cannot be criticized for is ignoring a substantial obligation.

Furthermore, I should also point out that in an increasingly interconnected and interdependent world the potential for relationships with distant others increases. One ambiguity in Reader's view is that it is not clear whether mutual dependence counts as a relationship. Increasingly, famine, poor health and environmental destruction in underdeveloped areas of the globe directly affect our wellbeing in the developed world, and our policies directly affect them. This is an ambiguity too complex to discuss in this context, but it may be that the idea of relationship must include connections of substantial mutual dependence as well.

The idea of grounding obligations in relationships makes sense of our intuitions in the examples of Pond and Overseas and blunts the criticism that we are inconsistent in our attitudes. In fact, this view explains a variety of well-entrenched moral judgements. The idea of relationship obligations is one we naturally apply in ordinary moral practice. I have a greater obligation to my wife than the institution at which I teach because I have a more extensive and personal involvement with her. I have a greater obligation to immediate family members than I have to a distant cousin because I am more extensively engaged with immediate family and there is a stronger biological connection. I have a greater obligation to a friend who has been a continual presence in my life than I have to a friend for whom I have great affection but see only occasionally. In other words, the strength of an obligation refers to the extent and depth of a relationship, although this is defeasible depending on the urgency of other demands to which we must respond. The stronger the obligation the more extensive and elaborate the range of behaviours and level of care that are required.

Despite the intuitive plausibility of this view, we still have to clarify the reasons for anchoring obligations in relationships, especially given the broad definition of relationships adopted here. Why do relationships give rise to obligations? How does the idea of a relationship obligation explain the authority and inescapability that obligations have? Furthermore, how is the idea of relationship obligation connected to the ethics of care? I began by arguing that, for an ethics of care, obligations arise out of feelings of care and connectedness with others. But we have many relationships with people we do not care about or care for. In fact, we unfortunately sometimes have relationships with some very bad people who may threaten us and do not invoke our sympathies at all. Why do we have obligations to them?

The answer to these questions requires an account of how relationships figure in our general orientation to the world. I will have more to say about this in the next chapter on happiness, but in order to clarify the nature of obligation we need to discuss the context of vulnerability that frames most human endeavour.

VULNERABILITY AND OBLIGATIONS

Human beings are connected to reality through a fundamental awareness of our vulnerability. From the first moments of consciousness, we are aware of needs and threats to the satisfaction of these needs. This vulnerability to loss is crucial to the development of our awareness of what has value, as I will argue in Chapter 5. We are vulnerable to loss of life, loss of the material goods we need to sustain life, we can lose our psychological stability and interest in the world, we can lose our prospects for the future, our self-respect, etc. And we are aware of these losses – they become an issue for us. Relationships help us cope with our vulnerability, with the fragility of human life. They help us secure and protect what we need to survive and flourish and thus themselves become our dominant need and continual source of value.

The understanding that we are bound up in relationships that enable us to cope with vulnerability is not a conclusion derived from evidence. Neither is it something we learn at school or in church, nor is it something we recognize when we properly attend to our long-term self-interest. We do not decide or discover the importance of relationships because we already dwell within them. They are the condition of our existence in much the same way that water conditions the existence of fish. Thus, our actions quite naturally take on ethical meanings to the extent they have some impact on the development and maintenance of relationships.

The ethical world is not something we have to reason ourselves into or find justification for, as if we start out life as independent individuals and then choose the relationships we want to pursue. All of us already exist in an ethical world, though we can develop habits and beliefs that make this world obscure. The upshot of this is that ethical meanings emerge out of the recognition of our fragility and limitations – the many ways we are vulnerable. It is no accident that most of the moral emotions are responses to loss. Guilt, shame, disgust, remorse, regret, indignation and compassion all presuppose that something of value has been diminished. The authority of morality is located here. Our vulnerability to loss exacts obedience from us, makes demands, and imposes constraints on our decisions and actions. The moral imperative comes from the deep-seated recognition that we are vulnerable, and only relationships enable us to cope with that vulnerability. Of course, relationships make us vulnerable as well; the loss of a relationship is one of the most serious losses we suffer. Part of what it means to become a good person is to learn to cope with this kind of vulnerability.

It follows from this, that any encounter involves seeing the other as needful. That is simply the way we look at the world. It is a basic recognition, as basic as recognizing the need for food and water, that other people rely on me and I rely on them. I rely on others in a very basic way – I rely on the assurance that you will not kill me, take my property, intentionally deceive me, etc. In some contexts, I rely on the assurance that I can count on your aid, solicitude or gratitude. Of course, much of this understanding is implicit, not fully articulated or made conscious. These understandings form the background of our interactions and we often attend to them only when they break down.

However, this reliance arises as an issue only when there is an encounter – a relationship of some sort. Only when people are in a relationship, broadly defined, can they be threatening or helpful. This fact provides us with a fuller recognition of the nature of moral authority. The other person in a relationship has the authority to command my commitment because her presence invokes the context of vulnerability that all of us share. She can be a threat or an aid to me – I can be a threat or an aid to her. I might not care about her in the sense of having a special relationship, but I must respond to her needs, either by ignoring them or taking them up. This is why Reader is correct to argue that obligations are grounded in relationships that require some point of contact to sustain them. Contact makes our vulnerability and the need for assurance stand out as important. Thus, in any encounter I am being commanded by the other to recognize her needs. However, whether I follow that command or not is another question. The command is not backed up by force – it only beckons.

Because we need to rely on others, stable relationships of various sorts are essential to human flourishing. But if relationships are to provide the context in which we can rely on others they must give assurance. In order for me to have that assurance, my needs must have some capacity to bind your will and your needs must have some capacity to bind my will. We provide this assurance in a variety of ways. Natural feelings of affection that characterize intimate relationships are perhaps the most prominent. These feelings help keep the welfare of our children, spouses and friends at the centre of our attention. We can sometimes transfer these feelings of affection to people with whom we have a less intimate relationship. Compassion and empathy can become generalized responses if we work hard at encouraging these feelings in ourselves.

Natural feelings of affection, as important as they are, nevertheless have limitations. Feelings are immediate responses to what is going on around us. They do not suffice as long-term assurances because they are changeable and easily disrupted by new stimuli or by emotions of disaffection such as anger or fear. Emotions are extraordinarily sensitive to detecting vulnerability and cannot always provide the assurance we require. This is true even in intimate relationships.

Thus, another way we provide for assurance is through the concept of obligation. Obligations secure the reliability of our actions. They use the authority of ethical meanings to bind my will to the needs of others and their will to my needs. The obligation to keep a promise assures the person to whom I made the promise that they need not adjust their expectations of how the future will unfold. The obligation not to kill without reason provides assurance even among strangers that we can sustain our encounter without fear of attack.

Some needs are so pervasive and shared by everyone that they are a permanent part of the way we respond to the world. Everyone always needs protection against loss of life, extreme suffering, abject humiliation, etc. There is never a moment in life when these are not fundamental needs. Given what we know about our vulnerability to loss of life, physical and psychological health, freedom, etc., we assign fundamental rights to all human beings that demand correlative obligations to protect those rights. This is what social contract theory was designed to establish, though the idea of a contract is an unnecessary abstraction. Other needs are no less important but less pervasive. I sometimes need to know the truth, but not always. I sometimes need people to keep promises, but not always, etc. Both categories of need, when brought to the surface by a relationship, impose obligations, though we usually do not describe the less pervasive type as the correlative of a right. In other words, there is no general right not to be lied to or to enforce the keeping of a promise because our needs in this regard fluctuate from moment to moment.

Given the role of vulnerability, we are now in a position to understand one source of moral necessity – one reason why some obligations are inescapable. In some relationships, characterized by actual connections, the degree to which others rely on us is so immediate and pressing, given their vulnerability, that to fail to respond would be a serious breach of our implicit understanding of the mutual assurances that enable us to survive and flourish. Conscience is just the felt recognition of the fragility of relationships, feelings that involve the horror and anguish of loosening the ties that regulate our exposure to vulnerability.

Of course, as I noted above, obligations have varying degrees of strength depending on the nature of the relationship. The strongest obligations arise only in situations of immediacy and importance. Thus, even basic relationships, such as an encounter with a stranger – the child in Pond – can impose a substantial obligation on a person. The need is immediate and terribly important. The obligation, though demanding because of the urgency of the need, may not be very extensive. We must rescue the child in Pond and ensure her safety but additional care will likely be beyond what duty requires. However, the more our lives are intertwined the greater the interdependence and the more extensive the obligations. We may be obligated to go out of our way to assist family members but strangers have less of a claim on our time and attention.

Importantly, we have obligations to non-persons since we have relationships with non-persons. Human life is dependent on a variety of animals, plants and artefacts that we dwell in the midst of, and the degree of involvement and interdependence as well as their susceptibility to loss imposes obligations on us. Relationships with pets and treasured objects invoke some of the same concerns regarding vulnerability that persons do, though to a lesser degree. We are vulnerable to their loss, they are valued but fragile, and the level of interaction is sufficient to establish a genuine relationship.

Philosophically, this account of obligation provides a variety of advantages. It explains the basic features of obligation by identifying the source of moral authority and explaining moral necessity. It provides a single criterion for determining the presence and extent of an obligation. One is obligated to the extent one is in a more or less full relationship with that to which one is obligated. This helps to ease some of the indeterminacy of moral particularism. Although contextual factors still come into play in determining what is important to attend to in a situation, the nature of the encounter determines the relative strength of moral properties, especially the degree of vulnerability and the immediacy of threats, and the depth of involvement with those whom we encounter in a context.

This account of obligation also provides us with some guidance on how to resolve conflicts between obligations. When obligations come into conflict, the obligation rooted in the fullest relationship takes precedence, although this priority can be defeated when judgements of importance and immediacy are overriding. The point at which judgements of importance and immediacy become overriding factors is too context-sensitive to be governed by a general rule. Thus, the basic insights of moral particularism are preserved, but we now know the sorts of considerations that can justify particular judgements.

Finally, this account of obligation satisfies the condition that we be able to live in accordance with our theories. It is in accord with our intuitive judgements about the conditions that obligate moral agents, and nothing in this account requires substantial modifications of human psychology. Relationship obligations need not disrupt identity-conferring commitments. In fact, they are responsive to such commitments, though the possibility of irresolvable conflict persists because our various commitments and obligations can come into conflict.

Relationship obligations also provide one plausible account of why Schindler felt it was necessary to risk his life to rescue his workers. As we know from Thomas Keneally's novel *Schindler's Ark* based on interviews with the Jewish workers he rescued, Schindler had extensive relationships with his workers that enabled him to see them as concrete individuals with intrinsic worth, and so vulnerable as to be thoroughly dependent on him. He was motivated by these specific workers at this particular time given the nature of the threat that all of them faced and the urgency of their plight. Apparently, their relationship imposed a demand on him that was impossible to ignore. Was his motivation primarily to respond to this demand? Or was there some idiosyncratic feature of his character that explains his capacity to respond as he did? There is no way to know the answer to this question although our discussion of qualities of character in Chapter 6 will help advance our understanding of Schindler's actions.

OBJECTIONS TO RELATIONSHIP OBLIGATIONS

Despite these advantages, however, before we can endorse this account of obligation, we must answer a variety of objections. If relationships give rise to obligations, do the obligations end when the relationship ends? Intuitively, if I have made a promise to a friend, I may still have an obligation to keep the promise if the friendship ends.

The answer to this objection depends on the specific obligation in question. In many cases, the end of a relationship does mean the end of obligations incurred because of the relationship. If I promise to attend a ball game with a friend, and the friendship ends, then the obligation need not be honoured. However, if I borrowed money from my friend, I would still owe the money despite the termination of the friendship. This is because the end of a friendship is not the end of all connections with that person who was my friend. We are connected to former friends by our shared history. The relationship is no longer a friendship, but it is no less a relationship. Thus, the obligation is still supported by a relationship and is still in force given the serious harm that results from the non-payment of debts.

One might also object that relationship obligations appear to make at least some actions that sustain or otherwise benefit a relationship obligatory, even though they may be harmful to others or to me. For instance, suppose that an employee of mine has done something to offend a close friend. In order to avoid alienating this valued but vengeful friend, I have to agree to fire the employee whose work has been exemplary. Intuitively, this action would be wrong even though it may help to sustain a relationship. We must explain that wrongness, but how can we if the moral quality of an action is wholly bound up with its role in the relationship with the deepest involvement?

This objection assumes that a single relationship determines the moral quality of an action. However, this is not the case. Harmful actions that nevertheless sustain a relationship can be wrong for reasons independent of that relationship. This is because we are involved in many relationships that make competing demands on us. To fire my employee in order to satisfy my friend's desire for revenge would be wrong, despite any demand my friend might place on me. This is because I also have relationships with employees that while less extensive, nevertheless, impose requirements on me, especially on an issue as urgent and important as someone's job. To fire an employee to satisfy a friend's vengeful feelings violates the obligation, based on my role as an employer, to treat employees fairly on matters of supreme importance.

THE LIMITS OF OBLIGATION

Some objections to the idea of relationship obligations involve ambiguities in what kinds of actions are obligatory. For example, the ethics of care suggests that we should seek to sustain relationships. Does that mean that we have an obligation to sustain them? If there is such an obligation to sustain relationships, what should we do about harmful relationships or relationships that no longer interest us?

Perhaps the most serious objection to relationship obligations is that some obligations appear to be independent of relationships; especially obligations to promote goods such as social justice. Don't we have an obligation to demand fair treatment even for those with whom we have no relationship? Shouldn't we try to advance the cause of justice for all persons regardless of our relatedness to them?

Both these objections assume too significant a role for obligations. Obligations play an important but limited role in our moral lives. It is important to see that many moral judgements do not produce obligations, and many moral prescriptions fall short of being obligatory.

The ethics of care does indeed recommend that we devote energy and attention to sustaining relationships. But this recommendation is not based on an obligation; it is based on our fundamental way of existing in the world. We form relationships because they are essential to leading a meaningful and flourishing life, not because they are obligatory. To the extent that our relationships prevent us from leading such a life, we have good reason to find new relationships, though some relationships may be so central to our conception of a meaningful life that they are difficult to discard. Obligations provide the assurances we need to engage in social life; they do not constitute social life.

Similarly, the directive that we should promote goods such as social justice is important, but not based on an obligation. We have an obligation to treat people we encounter fairly, and it is certainly praiseworthy and important that we demand that everyone be treated fairly. But this is because a good person ought to have qualities of character that enable her to take an interest in the lives of others. Apathy about the treatment of others, outside of a relationship as defined here, is a moral failure, but it is a failure of character, not a failure to honour an obligation. This point will become clearer in Chapters 5 and 6.

Remember that moral pluralism and moral particularism insist that many factors influence the moral quality of an action. The fact that an action is obligatory is only one of them. It is important in many contexts, but obligations are not necessarily more important than other factors such as whether an action exemplifies good qualities of character or personal ideals.

Moral theories that make the idea of obligation the most important moral consideration, such as deontological theories, have often been criticized for not taking a full range of character traits into consideration. A person, after all, could fulfil all of her obligations yet still not be a very good person. Imagine someone who always performs her obligations because they are required, but really dislikes having to consider the interests of others. So she is always grudging and unpleasant when co-operating, always does only what is barely necessary when carrying out an obligation, and although she always tells the truth and keeps her promises, she brags about doing so. This person would perform morally correct actions but would not be a very good person. To be good people we need to do more than honour obligations.

In this chapter, I have attempted to show that the people and things to which we are related make a claim on us. However, we still have to discover what enables us to take up that claim, and why it has such a priority. For this we need an account of moral character and happiness, the topics of the next two chapters.

REFERENCES AND SUGGESTIONS FOR FURTHER READING

Bentham, Jeremy (1988) [1789], *The Principles of Morals and Legislation*, Buffalo, NY: Prometheus.

Gauthier, David (1986), *Morals By Agreement*, Oxford: Oxford University Press.

Kant, Immanuel (1964) [1785], *Groundwork of the Metaphysics of Morals*, trans. H.J. Paton, New York: Harper and Row.

Keneally, Thomas (1982), *Schindler's Ark*, New York: Touchstone Press.

Rawls, John (1972), *A Theory of Justice*, Oxford: Oxford University Press.

Reader, Soran (2003), 'Distance, Relationship, and Moral Obligation', in *The Monist*, 86, 367–82.

Singer, Peter (1972), 'Famine, Affluence and Morality', in *Philosophy and Public Affairs*, 1, 229–43.

Smart, J.J.C. and Williams, Bernard (1973), *Utilitarianism: For and Against*, Cambridge: Cambridge University Press.

CHAPTER 5

HAPPINESS

We can conclude from the foregoing chapters that our capacities as moral agents are dependent on relationships, moral reason is pluralist and context-dependent, and that obligations are limited moral requirements based on the presence of actual connections between people that constitute relationships.

However, we have not said much about the kinds of relationships we should pursue, how we determine the standards of right and wrong that characterize our relationships, or what kinds of treatment beyond the minimal requirements of obligations will help us to flourish as human beings. In other words, we need a conception of what we should value and why. To complete the picture of morality, we need a vision of how to live that will make our moral lives intelligible. Once we decide what we want out of life and describe better and worse ways of living, we can then go about describing the qualities of character required to live a good life. Standards of right and wrong are natural by-products of this understanding of how to live.

Is there anything that all human beings want out of life that would give some structure and justification for our assignments of moral value? Any answer to this question is controversial, but one obvious candidate for something everyone wants is happiness. Of all the goods that human beings seek, happiness would seem to qualify as the ultimate aim.

The problem, of course, is that human beings disagree considerably about what counts as happiness. While I might think a life devoted to quiet contemplation is ideal, others may think a life devoted to military adventure is preferable, and still others think of happiness as nirvana or as receiving God's grace. When we look at the various pursuits people have organized their lives around, the variety seems endless. Furthermore, these different forms of life are likely to produce different conceptions of what counts as right or wrong. Thus, it is not obvious, on the face of it, how happiness can provide structure to our moral judgements given the variety of forms of life that count as happiness. Thus, before we can see how happiness provides structure to our assignments of value, we have to come up with a defensible definition of happiness and an account of how to achieve it.

The problem of defining happiness is not just an abstract, theoretical problem but a practical issue that most of us confront from time to time. Unfortunately, the nostrums and slogans in popular culture that harangue us about how to live do not provide reliable guidance. TV commercials encourage us to get the most out of life; but mum says we should be satisfied with what we have. 'If it feels good, do it' seems like a straightforward route to happiness if you can get away with it, but we are constantly reminded that what feels good is not necessarily good for us.

Furthermore, it seems as if the more success we have at creating the conditions for happiness, the less happy we are. Some social scientists have pointed out recently that the growth of material wealth in Western societies has not increased measures of subjective wellbeing. According to social scientist Barry Schwartz, since the 1970s the number of Americans describing themselves as very happy has declined by 5 per cent and the rate of clinical depression has increased substantially. It is fair to say that we are confused about happiness.

If we are to succeed in clarifying happiness, we will have to settle an issue that has persisted in discussions of happiness for centuries. That is the question of whether happiness is subjective or objective. The answer to this question is important for theoretical reasons, because it will significantly affect the ethical views that can be derived from the concept of happiness.

However, the question of whether happiness is subjective or objective is an important practical issue as well. If we are to find happiness, we have to know where to look for it. If happiness is subjective, we should look primarily to improving our psychological states, seeking personal satisfaction wherever possible and holding our own counsel when assessing the condition of our lives. But if happiness is not fundamentally a subjective matter, we may have to seek meaning beyond personal satisfaction, change the objective conditions in which we live, and strive to make our activity conform to an external standard. Is happiness a matter of attitude adjustment or social revolution?

HAPPINESS AND PLEASURE

In ordinary discourse, happiness usually refers to a positive psychological state. If someone were to ask you 'Are you happy?' you might respond, 'Yes, I'm happy; I just finished my final exams' or 'That was a wonderful meal.' The word 'happiness' often refers to a pleasurable experience. But if someone were to press the point and ask, 'Are you really happy, not just now but most of the time?' we might recognize that the person asking the question is looking for a deeper answer, one that identifies not just a current sensation but a long-term attitude towards one's life as a whole. One is happy in this deeper sense if one's life, overall, is going well. But what exactly is meant by 'going well'? Is it simply a collection of pleasing physiological sensations so if your life is filled with generally pleasurable experiences, you are happy?

The philosophical theory that endorses such a view of happiness is called hedonism. Hedonism equates happiness and pleasure and asserts that pleasure is the only thing in life that is good, the only thing worth pursuing. A life of happiness then would be a life that contains a favourable balance of pleasure over pain. From this account of happiness, it seems to follow that moral actions ought to cause pleasure and avoid pain.

This understanding of happiness is the basis for early utilitarian thought. Jeremy Bentham, the founder of utilitarianism, argued that pleasure is the ultimate aim of life and we should produce as much aggregate pleasure as possible. The problem is that it is not clear how we get a conception of moral value from hedonism given that a life of pleasure can be lived by an egregiously immoral person. Of course, utilitarians get around this by insisting that we adopt an objective point of view, in terms of which we consider the happiness of everyone equally. But as we saw in previous chapters, this is an unconvincing strategy.

Furthermore, many satisfying experiences that lead to happiness are not best described as pleasurable, because they do not involve physiological sensations. Being a parent or having a successful career are activities that include pleasurable as well as painful episodes, but the sense of overall satisfaction we typically gain from these activities is not itself a sensation. It may be immensely satisfying to recognize that occasionally there is justice in the world, but this recognition is not like an orgasm or a piece of chocolate. The satisfactions of parenting, having a successful career or admiring justice are attitudes rather than sensations and are directed towards general patterns in one's life rather than particular episodes.

Pleasant experiences by themselves do not qualify as happiness unless they contribute to a generally positive emotional tone that disposes us under appropriate circumstances to enjoy life. A person who experiences many intensely pleasurable experiences but is otherwise irascible or depressed is better described as generally unhappy. Although having pleasure in one's life is an important component in happiness, pleasure by itself does not have the emotional depth to constitute happiness. Thus, hedonism to be plausible must expand its account of pleasure to include long-term, stable dispositions to maintain, in the appropriate circumstances, positive emotions and moods.

However, even after stretching the hedonist's account of pleasure to include positive emotions and moods, hedonism still leaves out important dimensions of happiness. Happiness requires that we satisfy at least some of our most important desires. After all, a person could lead, on balance, a pleasant existence and sustain a generally positive emotional tone without ever satisfying her most important desires; but I doubt that we should call such a person happy. Someone who is constantly frustrated in her desires yet maintains a cheery demeanour is rightfully criticized as a 'Pollyanna' who is not sufficiently cognizant of her situation. She seems deluded, thinking she is happy without really being so.

For a final objection to hedonism, think back to the question that motivated this discussion of happiness. Often the question 'Are you happy?' refers not to a current psychological state but the condition of one's life generally, over a significant period of time. An affirmative answer to the question 'Are you happy in general?' requires an assessment of how the particular episodes in one's life add up, which produces an attitude of satisfaction towards one's life as a whole. Neither the assessment nor the resulting attitude is appropriately described as a pleasure.

Though having significant pleasures in one's life is part of happiness, happiness is a more comprehensive state involving a wide range of satisfactions – positive feelings, attitudes and judgements that are not pleasures. Thus, we can reject hedonism as a satisfactory account of happiness.

IS HAPPINESS SUBJECTIVE OR OBJECTIVE?

Throughout this discussion of hedonism, a plausible account of happiness has come into view. We can define happiness, at least initially, as the psychological disposition to maintain positive attitudes, moods and generally positive judgements towards one's life as a whole, all of which are explained by the satisfaction of our most important desires. Notice, however, that this definition of happiness emphasizes subjective elements of experience – psychological dispositions. This is happiness looked at from a first person point of view, how my life appears to me. The definition says little about whether certain objective conditions must be present in one's life to produce these psychological dispositions or whether the standards of assessment I use to judge my life happy are my own standards. If happiness is a subjective condition, then this is not a criticism of the above definition. However, if there are objective elements of happiness, then the above definition may be incomplete.

In one sense, any account of happiness must be subjective. 'Subjective' often means 'dependent on the mind' and contrasts with the idea of 'objective' as mind-independent. Happiness must be subjective in this sense. Happiness is, after all, something that we experience, and without a mind, we could not have experiences. However, the word 'subjective' also means that something is a matter of personal opinion – entirely dependent on the peculiarities of my mind or yours. Are the feelings, attitudes and judgements that constitute happiness largely up to me, or must they be responsive to something mind-independent?

There are two significant problems in defining happiness in terms of feelings, positive attitudes and satisfaction with one's life. Both problems stem from the subjective nature of this definition of happiness. The first problem has to do with the possibility that we can be mistaken in our assessments of happiness. Philosopher John Kekes argues that there is a substantial difference between feeling or judging that one is happy and really being happy. A person could have all of the positive attitudes and satisfactions that constitute happiness, but not be happy if these attitudes and satisfactions are based on illusions, deceptions or misinterpretations.

This view that we can be mistaken about our own happiness conflicts with many assumptions about happiness we make in practical circumstances. If a person says they are happy, we typically do not argue with them. After all, who is in a better position to determine whether one is happy or not than the person whose happiness is in question? However, although as a practical matter we often give people the benefit of the doubt about how they view their own lives, it is a serious mistake to think that individuals always have a firm handle on their own condition.

Suppose, for instance, a young woman reports that her life is extraordinarily happy. She has long wanted to be a lawyer and she has just received a law degree and has secured a job with a large firm. She has also recently married. Her husband is also a lawyer with similar career goals. Moreover, a central part of their bond is that they both agree that having a traditional, large family with lots of kids is the ideal to which they should aspire. Regardless of how she feels or her subjective evaluation of her situation, her conception of happiness can be criticized for being unrealistic and contradictory. It is unlikely that two people dedicated to the law can fully enjoy the benefits of having a large family. There is simply not enough time in the day. With regard to such a conception of happiness, we can predict a good deal of conflict and dissatisfaction.

Of course, they may find a way to balance their competing aspirations. The point is, this women's conception of happiness can be criticized. There are standards independent of her subjective conception of her condition to which the idea of happiness must conform. If we can be mistaken about our own happiness, then happiness is not a purely subjective matter, since the standards by which we judge happiness are not entirely up to the individual.

The Truman Show, a popular film released in 1998 starring Jim Carrey, illustrates the sense in which conceptions of happiness cannot be wholly subjective but must be rooted in reality. The good natured Truman Burbank is a happy man with a happy wife, living in the picturesque town of Seahaven, full of happy people who apparently have everything they need. Truman lives an ordinary, though highly idealized, life, in which everything works out for the best, and tragedy seems wholly out of place. At the beginning of the film, if someone had asked Truman if he was happy or not, he would surely have answered in the affirmative. Though Truman does not know it, he is, in fact, the main character in a live television show that runs 24 hours a day, his every move recorded by an arsenal of 5,000 cameras. Seahaven is a massive production studio sealed off from the rest of the world, and millions of people have watched every episode in Truman's life since his birth. His friends, wife and family, indeed everyone he meets, are really actors playing a fictional role in the drama.

Dramatic tension creeps into the narrative when Truman begins to notice odd occurrences that suggest things are not as they seem. As Truman frantically tries to uncover the mystery of his condition, the show's producers doggedly place obstacles in his path. When Truman finally uncovers the truth, he chooses to escape the confines of his manufactured reality, cheered on by the millions of viewers who have witnessed the final episode.

The point of this parable is that purely subjective criteria are not sufficient to justify judgements about happiness. Truman thought he was happy at least initially, but he was mistaken. His subjective feelings, positive mood and judgements about his personal satisfaction were fraudulent because they were not grounded in reality – they were manufactured, not caused in the appropriate way.

It is to be hoped that we are not so massively misled. *The Truman Show* is a product of Hollywood imagination rather than real life. But is it possible that some human beings are in an analogous situation – thinking they are happy but sadly mistaken? Before turning to that question, I want to point out another important fact about *The Truman Show*. Once Truman suspects that his happiness is based on an illusion, he struggles mightily to escape his condition. Why? If happiness is nothing but positive feelings and attitudes, why should he care whether the attitudes are based in reality or not?

When I test my student's intuitions about this and ask them if they would prefer a comfortable and prosperous life on *The Truman Show* to an ordinary life filled with many uncertainties, failures and hardships to overcome, most invariably choose an ordinary life and are appalled that anyone would take the alternative seriously. Why? Apparently, happiness must consist of something in addition to pleasant experiences and positive attitudes. Instead, these satisfying experiences must be the product of authentic attachments to reality in order to qualify as happiness.

The second problem with a thoroughly subjective account of happiness is that, because such a definition of happiness meets only a subjective standard, it cannot generate a moral point of view. A subjective account of happiness has little to say about how we should live our lives. A despicable person could have a variety of positive attitudes and satisfactions and thus be happy with no thought of morality at all. Morality would seem to play only a contingent role if one's desires happen to require co-operation of others.

Worries about the subjective character of happiness have led many thinkers, including Kant, to reject happiness as the source of morality. However, the need to overcome these objections to happiness as a subjective condition has encouraged other philosophers to seek a more objective account of happiness. Many have found insight and inspiration in the view of happiness held by the ancient Greek philosophers, especially Aristotle.

ARISTOTLE ON HAPPINESS

For Aristotle, all things in the universe have a purpose or end, and that purpose expresses the most complete form its nature can take. For instance, the purpose of an acorn is to become a thriving oak tree, just as the purpose of a harpist is to play the harp well. What is the purpose of a human being? There is a function specific to human beings, something that distinguishes us from all other beings. That function is reason and so our purpose must be to cultivate reason as best we can. Living life according to reason is our purpose and living an excellent life is to reason well and act accordingly. To achieve such a life is to achieve happiness. It is our ultimate purpose, the end to which all other goals are subordinate.

It follows from this that happiness, according to Aristotle, is not a feeling or a positive attitude. Instead, happiness is a life that is lived well according to objective standards for what counts as human flourishing. Just as through careful analysis of its nature, we can discover objectively what it means for a plant to flourish, we can also, through a careful analysis of human nature, discover objectively what it means for a human being to flourish. Happiness is therefore living that kind of flourishing life in which we let our rationality shine. The highest and fullest happiness would come from a life devoted to reason and contemplation because they are the highest expression of human potential.

Of course, there is more to our nature than rationality. We have emotions, desires and a variety of needs that we must satisfy. For Aristotle, in order to live a flourishing life, we have to develop all of our capacities and potential. The role of reason is to govern this process of development, to integrate our various capacities and direct them towards their perfection. If one leads a flourishing life, then one is likely to experience a good deal of pleasure and develop positive attitudes towards one's life. But these subjective elements are by-products of happiness, they do not define it. Happiness is not a state of mind. Rather, it is the condition of having fulfilled one's human potential.

Thus, for Aristotle, in order to be happy our activity must conform to our nature, and our nature is not something that we decide. Happiness refers to something independent of our subjective states. Nevertheless, it is something at which all of us aim. Though many of us are mistaken about the nature of happiness, its pursuit motivates all human activity. Aristotle's argument for this is that happiness is the only thing we want for its own sake. We do not want happiness in order to achieve something beyond happiness. It is good in itself. Every other activity or good is valuable because it produces happiness, and therefore these other goods are subordinate to it.

The virtue of Aristotle's view is that the concept of happiness can now generate a robust account of morality. In order for us to fulfil our potential, there are a variety of goods that we need. We need a degree of material wealth, good health, community status, knowledge, a degree of independence from the demands of others, etc. Above all, we must live in a well-functioning community. Without these sorts of goods, we cannot fulfil our potential.

However, in order to achieve these goods, we must develop the virtues. Virtues are dispositions – acquired habits – to act in ways that are conducive to developing our potential. Unlike plants and other natural objects, human beings can choose to deviate from their nature. Thus, we have to train ourselves in the pursuit of happiness by developing the virtues that enable us to fulfil our potential.

Aristotle divides the virtues up into intellectual and moral virtues. Intellectual virtues involve the capacities required in order to understand the universe in which we live – essentially the ability to do maths and science. Practical wisdom is also an intellectual virtue. Practical wisdom is the ability to appreciate what is good and bad for human beings and the ability to apply this knowledge in particular circumstances in order to direct our actions towards the achievement of happiness. Moral virtues are habits of character that express themselves in the correct emotional response to any situation we might confront. The correct emotional response aims at the midpoint between two extremes, one extreme involving too much emotion, the other extreme involving too little emotions. Our practical wisdom identifies what the proper midpoint is.

Thus, for instance, Aristotle lists courage as a virtue. The ability of a person to act with courage is determined by the degree to which we can control our fear. Courage involves having the right amount of fear in a situation. If I experience too much fear, I am a coward. Cowardice is a vice. If I experience too little fear in a situation, I am foolish and reckless. Being reckless is a vice. Having the virtue of courage involves having just the right amount of fear, appropriate to the circumstances. A virtue is thus a mean between two extremes, the midpoint between two vices, which Aristotle refers to as the golden mean.

The role of practical wisdom is to control the emotions so our actions habitually hit the mean. Virtues become part of our character when our reason properly moulds our desires and emotions to respond correctly in any situation. To act in accordance with virtues, of course, takes a great deal of practice and trial and error. There are no rules that help us and what counts as virtuous will change from situation to situation and from person to person. Only a person with much experience and training can become adept at striking the right emotional balance.

As a consequence, unlike deontological and utilitarian theories, we cannot determine what is right independently of what a virtuous person would do. This is why the evaluation of persons is more important than the evaluation of actions for Aristotelians. When deciding what to do, the appropriate question is not 'What is right?' but is instead 'What would a good person do?' It also means we cannot determine what the right thing to do is by following a rule. We must have the proper motives and dispositions and we must exercise them in ways that conform to the situations in which we act.

Aristotle, thus, provides an interesting way of answering a question I posed in Chapter 1. How can the interests of someone else become a reason for me to act if I don't share those interests? Why should I tell the person buying my car that it leaks oil and she will have to add a quart once a week? Aristotle's answer is that I may not have a reason to provide information that might cost me money, but I do have a reason to acquire virtues that will lead to happiness. Thus, once I acquire the motivation to act virtuously, the intelligibility of altruistic actions is not dependent on an immediate desire. Honesty is an expression of what I am, not what I want. Thus, I should tell the truth because it is important to maintain one's character.

Aristotle lists a variety of qualities of character that count as virtues. In addition to courage, he includes honesty, justice (treating others according to what they deserve), the enjoyment of pleasure in moderation (temperance), generosity, spending lavishly and entertaining well (magnificence), pride, honesty, good temper, capacity for shame, etc. Unfortunately, some virtues do not fit the neat scheme of the golden mean. Aristotle grants that murder and assault are always wrong – there is no degree of murder that is just right. It is always wrong to feel envy and spite; you can never have too much justice. Aristotle's scheme for identifying virtues is thus incomplete. Nevertheless, the idea is intuitive and appealing. If we develop all of the virtues as habits that become permanent parts of our character, we have the best chance of being happy over the course of a lifetime.

Some of these virtues might strike you as being less than essential. Is throwing a good party essential for happiness? Furthermore, Aristotle leaves many virtues off the list that we might think are essential in modern societies. Modern conceptions of fairness and tolerance do not appear. Similarly, he does not mention the qualities one needs to be effective in the workplace. This is because fairness, tolerance and industriousness were not essential for Greek aristocrats like Aristotle. Apparently, throwing a good party was important. This highlights the fact that what counts as a virtue is dependent on the sort of goods one wants to achieve. Different packages of goods will produce different lists of virtues, although I suspect that some virtues such as honesty, courage and justice would appear on almost any list of virtues.

Aristotle includes one more element in his conception of happiness – good luck. Happiness is available only to those who are fortunate enough to live in a society in which the virtues can be trained properly. If someone has the misfortune of being unable to acquire the virtues, they cannot achieve the goods required for happiness.

Aristotle's theory is appealing because it is a practical philosophy that takes seriously the entire human personality. Ethics is not opposed to human happiness, as it seems to be for Kant, or opposed to my personal happiness and integrity as for the utilitarian, but is an integral part of the pursuit of happiness. When we act rightly, it is not because we have ignored our desires, but because we have trained our desires to pursue what is in our nature to pursue. However, Aristotle's claim to have specified what must count as an ideal life for human beings is questionable. Aristotle argues that to be a good person is to perform the functions of a person well, and he thinks that we can give an objective account of human functioning – namely the capacity to reason, which is described in terms of the intellectual virtues and practical wisdom. Values are simply a natural product of what we are.

The problem is that many activities are uniquely human – creative and artistic pursuits, athletic activities, technological development, humour, social activities, etc. Any of these can claim to be central to human functioning. Many of these will require a variety of skills and capacities but moral virtue may not be essential to them, or may require only a minimal commitment to morality rather than moral excellence. Many of them will require certain cognitive capacities but not necessarily those concerned with the pursuit of knowledge or practical wisdom. For instance, a person could make good use of her skill as a basketball player but make middling use of her reasoning ability. Why is that person not functioning well according her own developmental capacities? She must reason well enough to get by, but does not require excellence in that regard.

Aristotle also thinks that we ought to be moderate in our pursuit of pleasure. But for a person with a discriminating palate, why should he be moderate in his pursuit of excellent food and wine? To use moderation in this pursuit would be to compromise his characteristic function. And how much courage does such a person require? Surely, in many circumstances, the risk averse can lead happy lives. The connections between a good life and the moral and intellectual virtues are not as tightly woven as Aristotle thought.

Thus, Aristotle does not provide a defensible view of an ideal life. When we look at the lives that human beings tend to choose, there are many candidates for a good life that require different packages of goods. Moreover, even if we did come up with a single account of an ideal life, we would still not want to say that someone who cannot meet it could not be happy. This is because happiness clearly does involve some subjective elements. Intuitively, we want to say that a disabled person who lacks some human capacities can nevertheless be happy. Aristotle's view cannot explain why someone with limited abilities, who cannot lead an ideal life, could nevertheless be happy. Similarly, a very competent and successful person, who is fulfilling her potential, may be deeply unhappy from a subjective point of view, a possibility that Aristotle seems to ignore.

A theory of happiness that leaves out the subjective element entirely would run up against the following hurdle. Clearly, the subjective aspects of happiness motivate us; we seek happiness in part because the positive feelings and satisfactions are so important to us. The pursuit of happiness can explain so much of human behaviour because the positive feelings and satisfactions are so important to us. If we discount the subjective elements, it is not obvious that the pursuit of happiness can be the motive it is alleged to be.

Aristotle's theory has not provided us with an objective foundation for morality. However, he does provide us with an outline of what such an account might look like. As human beings, we have a variety of aims and goals that we pursue. In that pursuit, there are better and worse ways of achieving goals. Though the basketball player may not reason excellently, she must play well and there are reasonably objective ways of measuring her ability. For the connoisseur of fine food, he may not require moderation or more than minimal courage, but as a judge of good taste he must be fair in his evaluations. Aristotle is right to emphasize the fact that if we are to realize the goods that we seek, we must develop the qualities of character that enable us to acquire them. There are many things worth pursuing and some activities will not count as pursuing them well. Thus, despite the fact that there is no ideal form of human life, we can judge many activities to be inconsistent with our aims. We must cultivate the virtues that are internal to our practices, and that provides a starting point for criticism and evaluation.

To sum up, we have looked at happiness as consisting of subjective feelings of pleasure, positive attitudes and the satisfaction of one's main desires. But that position cannot accommodate the possibility of being mistaken about our judgements of happiness or the recognition that our experiences must be authentic in order to contribute to happiness. The attitudes and experiences themselves do not constitute happiness unless they are explained by our capacities as functioning human beings in the real world. We then looked at happiness as an objective condition of flourishing where happiness is grounded in the exercise of our highest human capacities objectively determined. But that view implausibly narrows the realm of what counts as a worthwhile goal for human beings. Furthermore, it leaves out the personal dimension of happiness, which is essential if happiness is to supply a motive for our actions. Neither the subjective nor the objective theory of happiness is complete, although both have their virtues.

HAPPINESS IN CONTEXT

An adequate theory of happiness must explain why happiness is more than simply feeling good about life, but it must not sacrifice the importance of those positive feelings and attitudes that are obviously central to happiness. I think we can make some progress on developing such a theory if we understand happiness as a pattern of activity and judgement through which we enjoy the worth of that about which we care. Happy people are engaged in a world of people, things and activities they care about, and they are able to enjoy that caring. Our enjoyment of that which has genuine value enables the moods, attitudes and satisfactions that we call happiness. In other words, positive attitudes and satisfactions are a by-product of the capacity to enjoy a world suffused with value.

This view differs from Aristotle's in that it does not define happiness in terms of an ideal. Happiness is, in part, a summary judgement about the way the episodes in our lives extract value from the situations in which we find ourselves. It does not demand that our situation take a particular shape. Thus, this view explains something that Aristotle's theory could not – why people of ordinary ability or some disability often report being happy even under dire conditions. Because happiness is not about fulfilling an ideal but is instead about responding to what has value in our situation, the achievement of happiness is possible under a wide variety of conditions. This view also explains why people with rapidly rising expectations under conditions of plenty, as well as people who are enormously successful, can nevertheless be unhappy – they have not yet learned to grasp what is of genuine value in their circumstances. Thus, this view does not have the defects of Aristotle's position.

However, on first reading it seems that this alternative does not differ sharply from the subjectivist view. If happiness is a pattern of activity through which we enjoy the worth of that which we care about, then what we choose to care about and the attitudes we take towards these concerns seem to be subjective matters. Why couldn't the character in *The Truman Show* satisfy my definition by choosing to care about and enjoy the ersatz episodes thus achieving happiness?

The answer to these questions is that care cannot be construed as thoroughly subjective without making a mystery of what it means for something to matter to us. In other words, the positive feelings and attitudes that we normally associate with happiness count as happiness only if they are produced by our interactions with things of genuine value. And what counts as having genuine value is not a thoroughly subjective affair.

To begin to understand why our capacity to discover value cannot be wholly subjective, think about the range of things you care about. Think about when they began to have value for you. Did you consciously choose to begin to care about them? Did you manufacture or dream up this interest? Obviously, some of our interests are the product of conscious decisions – one can decide to pursue an interest in basketball or chemistry. But for the most part with regard to what we care most deeply about we simply find ourselves with these concerns. Our interest in them is not fully under our control.

Much of what we care about makes up a set of background conditions that give structure to how we think and feel but are not the subject of conscious deliberation and choice. Our physical makeup, bodily orientation and perceptual and motile abilities structure our experience of the world as well as our self-conceptions and help to determine what we do with our lives. We do not decide to have excellent eye-hand co-ordination or perfect pitch. Psychological and behaviour patterns are not chosen either. We do not decide to be the kind of person who is easily angered or who remains calm in an emergency. Our abilities as social beings – to be assertive or passive, extroverted or introverted, etc. – develop long before we have much control over them. Yet, these patterns influence significantly how we live. The meaning of sexual and gender orientations are largely determined by social patterns and institutions, yet these have a great deal to do with how we determine life plans, preferences and habits, including the type of person with whom we will be romantically connected. Though deliberation and choice shape some of these factors, for the most part these patterns of behaviour are simply given – relatively fixed factors in our lives that we discover about ourselves and cannot without difficulty be altered.

Moreover, the way these abilities and capacities engage the world matter to us; the activities they make possible have a kind of familiarity that is intrinsically part of us. Importantly, their exercise is inherently satisfying and our ability to exercise them and to enjoy that exercise plays a significant role in whether we our happy or not.

Many of our emotional attachments are facts that guide our lives but are not subject to our control in any significant way. Our feelings towards our parents or other family members are products of a history that began long before we could deliberate about things and make choices, and they have become settled parts of our lives. Parents do not decide to love their children – it just happens and is seldom up for reconsideration. For most people, though not all, their racial and cultural identities are fixed facts that are not open to modification. Most people have some basic value commitments that are so fundamental to their identity or way of life that they have never deliberated about them or cannot seriously consider rejecting them.

Thus, the way the world matters to us is not something that we aim for or decide but something we already are. The things that have value and the standards by which we judge their value are not solely a product of my will or deliberation. This is not to say that our decisions and deliberation play no role in what we value. Rather, our decisions require as their background a world of value that we are already engaged in from which our decisions gain meaning and significance.

As the twentieth-century German philosopher Martin Heidegger argued, the structure of care constitutes our 'being in the world' into which we are 'thrown'. The situation in which each of us finds ourselves has an aspect of 'givenness' to it to which we must respond. Many of our values confront us as facts about us just as inevitably as our height, eye colour or DNA patterns.

Thus, to the extent happiness has to do with seeing the world as valuable, it is misleading to think of happiness as thoroughly subjective, something that is up to us to determine. The subjective view leaves out of the picture the sense that the natural and social context in which we are situated has a claim on us, shapes and influences us and demands that we respond to it, prior to us reflecting on it or making decisions about how we want to be situated. And this pre-reflective situatedness strongly influences not only our prospects for happiness, but the judgements and attitudes we use to evaluate our lives as happy or not.

To avoid misunderstanding, I want to emphasize that I am not claiming that we have no control over what we value. We have substantial control over what we care about, but this control operates against a background of capacities and commitments that we do not choose. The general point of this discussion is that, if we are to be happy, we must respond to our situation in ways that produce the dispositions and attitudes associated with happiness. If our attitude or judgements about our happiness are not responsive to salient features of our condition and circumstances, we can be criticized for this lack of fit. We can fail to be genuinely happy.

However, the degree of fit between our subjective assessment of our situation and the conditions under which we live leaves a great deal of latitude for our creative responses. Human beings are remarkably flexible in the ways we respond to situations. Nevertheless, there are constraints on how our judgements and attitudes must conform to the shape of reality.

These constraints largely have to do with our vulnerability to loss. Remember that on the definition of happiness we are working with, happiness involves a judgement that my world and my activity has value, a judgement that is reflected in my attitude towards my life. Part of what it means to value something is to be concerned about its loss. When we care deeply about something, our attitude is in part a product of the recognition that it can disappear or be destroyed. Although something may be of value because of its intrinsic properties, vulnerability to loss enhances its value. This is why rare goods are expensive. Diamonds are beautiful but would not be worth much if they were readily accessible. The same is true of non-material goods. Losing a loved one is painful because it is the loss of something irreplaceable. No one else can be an adequate substitute. Though we may develop positive attitudes and feelings of pleasure towards things that are replaceable or plentiful, these attitudes typically do not have the emotional depth of our attitudes towards things that are vulnerable.

Thus, to have things of value in one's life is to be surrounded by things that are vulnerable. Their vulnerability in part makes them valuable. The upshot of this argument is that happiness does not arise from making ourselves invulnerable to loss since that would reduce the value in our lives. Rather, happiness requires that we acknowledge our vulnerability and successfully cope with it through developing attitudes of care. An attitude of care for things of value is not an optional attitude we can adopt or not. Care, in the sense of a nurturing attitude that sustains value, is essential to happiness.

However, the degree to which something or someone is vulnerable is not thoroughly within our control. In matters of life, death, scarcity and abundance, the world is not always responsive to our wishes. To the extent our happiness is dependent on enjoying that about which we care, our prospects for happiness are not subjective and neither are our judgements about happiness. In other words, given what I care about, whether I am able to enjoy the value in my situation is not entirely up to me.

This dependence of our attitudes towards things we value on perceptions of vulnerability explains why most of us would decline to continue with *The Truman Show* despite the offer of secure satisfactions. In a purely fantasy-driven world in which nothing is at risk, our deep sense of involvement with things that arises from their vulnerability would be absent. We might get pleasure from our activities but they would not be significant enough to induce the long-term attitudes and dispositions we associate with happiness. Assignments of value would be tentative and unstable at best. Surely, we would perceive that as a loss.

In summary, to be happy is to make what is valuable part of one's life. To value something is, in part, to perceive it to be vulnerable. Thus, to be happy is to actively sustain that which is vulnerable. The positive attitudes that constitute happiness are by-products of this ability to sustain value. In order to achieve this we must adopt an attitude of care towards that which can be destroyed. Happiness is achievable only when we develop caring responses to the reality we are given.

This shows that our assignments of value are typically dependent on our perception of our limitations as human beings, perceptions that are regulated by our actual situation. Take away those limitations and it is hard to imagine what it means to value something. This is why the subjective view of happiness makes a mystery of what it means to value something.

Thus far I have been concerned to show that the positive attitudes and affirmative judgements about life that make up happiness must be rooted in genuine sources of value that cannot be described as wholly subjective. However, positive attitudes that our caring responses generate are only one component of happiness, because these positive attitudes also depend on judgements that we make about how our lives are going. Happiness involves a judgement of approval about one's life, a judgement that most of our wants are being satisfied, and that our wants are worth having. This requires having a view about what one's life should be. What standards do we use when we make such an approving judgement? Is this judgement the sort of thing about which we can be mistaken?

The appropriate standard is the degree to which we are able to enjoy the value that exists in our situation. Happiness depends on how attentive, engaged and responsive we are to the sources of genuine value in our midst. When we succeed, in those situations that have significance, in realizing the potential for enjoyment we are justified in claiming happiness. The word 'enjoyment' here is a term of art. I mean by it an appreciation of what is beneficial, virtuous, healthful, beautiful, admirable, authentic – we could continue the adjectives indefinitely but the gist is clear. When, through our actions and attention, we succeed in making the good that is available to us persistently visible in our lives, we are justified in asserting our happiness.

By contrast, a person who recognizes that there are things and activities of value available to her but also recognizes that she persistently cannot make them part of her life, she is judging her life to be unhappy. When people claim there is something missing in their lives they are implicitly recognizing the gap between what could be and what is. Thus, a person who is wealthy and successful may be unhappy, not because wealth and success are bad but because she may lack the dispositions to appreciate the goods that wealth and success bring. Success may yield an address book full of contacts but if she finds no delight in these relationships or fails to uncover the strengths and vitality of the people with whom she interacts, they will not contribute to happiness. Wealth enables the purchase of a well-engineered luxury car, but if she understands nothing of the pleasures and challenges of fine engineering it will quickly seem like a hollow purchase when the novelty wears off. Most importantly, if the achievement of wealth and success is not accompanied by the sense that it is hard won and easily lost it will lose some of its appeal because the sense of vulnerability that underlies all value is missing. By contrast, a person of modest means may be quite happy if she is able to discover the richness of a friend's personality or appreciate the historical lustre of a well-worn roadster.

Thus far, I have been arguing that happiness consists of positive attitudes and dispositions that are caused by our capacity to care for what has value in one's life. There is one additional element essential to happiness. Our judgements about happiness are not judgements about individual episodes in a life, but are summary judgements that evaluate life as a whole. One of our deepest desires is to be satisfied with life overall, not merely as a series of distinct episodes. Thus, in addition to the judgement that I am successful at making what I care about part of my life, happiness requires a judgement that doing so is what links my past, present and future. The judgement that happiness is a persistent, long-term element in life is part of happiness. However, if this is the case, there must be some recognizable feature of life that explains this persistence. What enables us to make the value of our relationships and activities a continuous element in our lives?

I want to suggest that identity-conferring commitments play this role. Some things that we value become essential to who we are, so that we could not give them up without severe psychological trauma. They provide a centre that lends structure and coherence to our lives. The range of things to which human beings are able to attach such significance is immeasurably large. Attachments to family, friends, professions, artistic and athletic pursuits, religion, material gain, pleasures of all sorts, etc., can be the source of identity-conferring commitments. In any case, these attachments enable us to discover what has value for us over the long run. Identity-conferring commitments provide the perspective from which we can evaluate life as a whole. If we are able to sustain these commitments and enjoy that caring, then we are justified in asserting long-term happiness. To summarize, happiness requires the following elements:

a. Long-term dispositions to maintain positive attitudes and feelings that are caused by:
b. The enjoyment of what has value in one's life supported by caring responses; and
c. A judgement that one is enjoying what has value (in other words, happiness involves the recognition that one is happy); and
d. Identity-conferring commitments that support the judgement that one is happy over the long run.

I call this conception of happiness 'voluptuous care' – a mode of being in the world in which we make what is valuable to us a persistent element in our lives.

Above, I argued that the positive attitudes and feelings associated with happiness are not thoroughly subjective. I also argued that happiness is a matter of making what we care about a persistent part of our lives. What about the judgements of approval we make towards our lives? Is it up to each one of us to determine the standard for what counts as a happy life?

The judgement of approval involved in happiness must be an assessment of how one is doing in recognizing what is of value in one's situation and in appreciating the worth of that which is available, which requires balancing competing goods so that the value of each can be appreciated. We could be mistaken about either assessment.

Every choice we make regarding what to value and how much to value it involves an opportunity forgone. In choosing one career, we make it impossible to pursue alternative careers. In choosing to spend time with family, we compromise the quality of our work, etc. Thus, nearly every significant choice involves some loss. If we are attentive, we cannot avoid the sense that an experience not fully experienced magnifies the losses. Sometimes, the loss is irretrievable; the permanent loss of something valuable is one of the most profound of human experiences, and it regulates our moods and attitudes. This is an unavoidable consequence of value pluralism; there are many things to care about and limited resources to nurture them all.

Consequently, the judgements of approval that happiness requires must be judgements that the gains outweigh the losses; and these judgements can sometimes be wrong. We can fail to acknowledge what we care about or fail to pay attention when values are compromised. We can self-deceptively pretend we did not care anyway when suffering a loss, or fail to transform what we care about into identity-conferring commitments that make long-term happiness possible. When we adopt these mistaken strategies, happiness surreptitiously slips away without our knowing it. To devalue our fundamental values is to deny the constancy required for the judgement that our lives over the long run are happy. The lament that 'I thought I was happy, but it was an illusion' is not uncommon. It expresses the fact that happiness reaches beyond our subjective states.

In order to achieve happiness, it is essential to maintain connection to things of value. To flourish is to find sustained meaning in one's activities and in one's relationships. To care about what is vulnerable is not an optional form of life that we can take or leave. It is our fundamental way of being in the world. The human task is to find meaning in the world, and when we engage in activities that inhibit that task our lives and the lives of others are diminished.

Two caveats are important to avoid misunderstanding. One way of glossing this account is that happiness is a matter of learning to accept the situation you are in and get the most out of it. But this gloss would be misleading. One might be in a situation in which there are few sources of value, nothing that attracts deep commitment or that warrants emotional or cognitive investment. Or one's situation, although satisfactory, may contain few prospects for growth, thus making stable, relatively long-term judgements of approval difficult to sustain. Happiness would likely be unavailable to a person in such circumstances.

Furthermore, the idea of getting 'the most' from what we value is not an ideal available to human beings. Most human beings value a variety of different goods and many of these goods are in conflict or mutually incompatible. For instance, I may value my job and my family, but to get 'the most' out of my job would entail substantial compromise in time and energy devoted to family. Thus, to extract enjoyment from both job and family I have to find a balance that enables me to grasp the richness of both without demanding that I maximize my enjoyment of either. Thus, happiness requires that our circumstances are at least minimally fortunate and that we are capable of making reasonable trade-offs between the variety of things we care about.

We still have to understand how happiness as voluptuous care generates a moral point of view. For that we need a discussion of the qualities of character required for happiness, a topic we will turn to in the next chapter. Nevertheless, this discussion of happiness helps pull together a variety of themes raised in earlier chapters.

In earlier chapters, we have seen that capacities for moral agency and moral reasoning, as well as the authority of obligations, rest on relationships. But if these claims are to be fully intelligible we must place relationships in a larger context. We form relationships because they are essential to leading a meaningful and flourishing life. They are essential for our happiness. Our connections to other people are the most vulnerable relationships we have and our feelings and judgements about the quality of our lives are dependent on sustaining those relationships.

At the end of Chapter 4, we saw that obligations are only one among a variety of moral considerations. The others arise out of our interest in happiness. Most of our intimate relationships are governed only minimally by obligations and more by deep feelings of care and connectedness that, to a significant extent, provide assurance through natural feelings of trust. These relationships, and the moral norms that regulate them, are intelligible because of our interest in happiness.

Though there is more to say about moral reasoning in the next chapter, this account of happiness helps clarify the process of moral reasoning described in Chapter 3. We make judgements about the relative strength of moral properties in a context against the background of our pursuit of happiness. To flourish is to find sustained meaning in one's activities and relationships, and we judge our actions in light of this need. Certainly, we judge our actions against the background of perceived vulnerability. Attentional focus and conceptual discrimination are a function of what we care about, and what we care about is a function of perceptions of vulnerability. The standard of correctness we use in such judgements is the degree to which an action enables us to make something of value part of our lives. Relationships that contribute to our sense of meaning and value, even when they are demanding or difficult, are worth preserving. But relationships that do not contribute to our sense of meaning and value have a diminished status, and thus a diminished claim on our time and attention, subject of course to the demands of obligation.

Recall from Chapter 3, that one difficulty with the ethics of care is that it may be too demanding unless we can specify when it is permissible to refuse to care for someone. We have a general response to that worry. The pursuit of happiness constrains our decisions about how to distribute our caring resources, since some caring activities will be incompatible with the need to sustain our pursuit of value and meaning. Our caring responses, if they are to be intelligible, must not violate the livability criterion. There are limits to care as a moral requirement.

Happiness as voluptuous care also brings our common humanity into the picture. Although each person has a unique perspective and confronts unique obstacles, all human beings share certain vulnerabilities that define the limit conditions of human existence. All human beings must deal with mortality, limited knowledge and resources, and biological and social constraints. Because of these shared vulnerabilities, the experiences of others are seldom so opaque that understanding is impossible. Although there are many forms of life that enable human beings to flourish, we can make defensible judgements about whether a form of life deals well or badly with the limit conditions of human existence.

Finally, this account of happiness brings Schindler's actions more sharply into focus. The extreme vulnerability of Schindler's workers and his relationship with them left Schindler with little choice but to attempt an elaborate rescue operation. A refusal to rescue would have put Schindler in the position of denying something of extraordinary value. We should not underestimate the cost of subtracting so much of value from one's life. Had Schindler not done what he did, he might have been crushed by his judgements about how he was doing in enjoying the things of value in life. His happiness was at stake. Of course, he could have chosen differently and discovered something else to value. But not without suffering a loss. What might have compelled Schindler to decide that such a loss was not worth suffering? To answer this question we have to see how qualities of character fill out a moral point of view.

REFERENCES AND SUGGESTIONS FOR FURTHER READING

Aristotle (1985), *The Nicomachean Ethics*, trans. Terence Irwin, Oxford: Oxford University Press.

Bentham, Jeremy (1988) [1789], *The Principles of Morals and Legislation*, Buffalo, NY: Prometheus.

Heidegger, Martin (1962), *Being and Time*, trans. John Macquarrie and Edward Robinson, New York: Harper and Row.

Kekes, John (1982), 'Happiness' in *Mind*, vol. 91, 358–76.

McFall, Lynn (1989), *Happiness*, New York: Peter Lang.

Mill, John Stuart (1969) [1863], *Utilitarianism*, ed. J.M. Robson, Toronto: University of Toronto Press.

Schwartz, Barry (2004), 'The Tyranny of Choice', in *The Chronicle of Higher Education*, vol. 50, issue 20, B6.

Sumner, Wayne L. (1996), *Welfare, Happiness, and Ethics*, Oxford: Clarendon Press.

CHAPTER 6

QUALITIES OF MORAL CHARACTER

The previous chapters leave some fundamental questions unanswered. What cognitive and emotional processes do we use to make reliable moral judgements? What does it mean to be guided by what one cares about? How should we resolve conflicts between obligations and between obligations and other moral concerns? What activities does care entail? Since obligation makes up only a portion of morality, what other specific considerations play a role in moral reflection?

Answers to these questions will require that we provide an account of what it means to be a good person. This question has never been far from our discussion. But we have been discussing it indirectly, in part because much of traditional moral theory treats it as a secondary issue. Utilitarianism and deontology focus on what actions are morally right or wrong. They define a good person as a person who performs right actions and avoids wrong ones, and direct their attention to defining right action. But the ethics of care begins to shift this discussion because right acts are defined as actions that emerge from certain motives, namely those that exhibit care. Thus, in the ethics of care, the idea of a caring person is primary, and conceptions of right or wrong action are derived from that.

The ethics of care is therefore closely related to what has come to be known as virtue ethics. Rather than focus on actions, virtue ethics seeks moral guidance by developing a model of a good person and the character traits that make up a good person. These traits are called virtues or qualities of character. Given the limitations of utilitarianism and deontology, virtue ethics, which relies on the Ancient Greek and Hellenistic philosophers for inspiration and insight, has in recent years received a good deal of attention. The virtue approach is appealing because overall assessments of character are important to us. We do not evaluate persons simply by looking at their actions; we look at their motives as well and a person who does the right thing but has the wrong motive is subject to criticism. Furthermore, as noted in previous chapters, many qualities of character and the actions that flow from them are not generated by an obligation. A good person may be cautious, cheerful, co-operative, sincere, committed, friendly, courteous, compassionate, full of gratitude, civil, caring, and may stand up for what they believe without being obligated to do anything. A morality based on obligations fails to cover a large area of our moral lives.

What qualities of character or virtues are necessary for a person to be good? By 'good person,' we mean something in addition to merely possessing admirable qualities. We might admire someone with baseball skill, intelligence or a sense of humour, but such a person would not necessarily be a good person. 'Good person' usually refers to someone who is morally good. How do we specify which qualities to include under the category of moral goodness? As I noted in the last chapter, qualities of moral character or virtues are usually components of conceptions of happiness. There are far too many virtues to discuss in this brief introduction. The question for us is what are the most important qualities required for happiness as voluptuous care. I will discuss three virtues – care, integrity and practical wisdom – but keep in mind that this list is not exhaustive.

CARE AS A VIRTUE

The concept of care discussed in Chapter 5, loosely based on the work of Heidegger, is not a quality of character. Rather it is a philosophical term that names the way human activity in general acquires meaning. Care is part of the basic structure of human experience, not a quality that a person may or may not have.

However, the ethics of care does rely on a more familiar use of the word care that is appropriately called a virtue. And the two uses of care are connected as I will argue shortly. Think of care in this more ordinary sense as a disposition to nurture and preserve what has value. Care is aimed at particular people or things with which a moral agent has an intimate relationship. I will focus on care devoted to people, although an analysis of care devoted to things or animals is also important.

Care devoted to persons involves what Nels Noddings calls 'engrossment and motivational displacement'. 'Engrossment' means coming to grasp another person's reality from the inside, on her own terms rather than how we prefer to see her. It also involves an openness to being changed by the other. 'Motivational displacement' means that the caring person adopts the goals of the cared for and helps to promote them at least indirectly.

Engrossment and motivational displacement entail that a caring person has intimate knowledge of the person cared for, because a caring person's actions must be appropriate to the needs of the person receiving care. Because caring relationships involve some degree of intimacy, there is often an emotional element in care. The caring person is concerned for the needs and aspirations of the person cared for. Thus, she will feel pleasure when things are going well and disappointment or sadness in difficult times; she will enjoy the activities of caring when possible but also share the pain if suffering is involved. Importantly, if care is a virtue along the lines of Aristotle's conception, a caring person must engage in activities willingly and spontaneously. But the emotional element need not be present since many caring activities are mundane or routine and thus lack the elements that stimulate feelings.

Care qualifies as a virtue because it is related in the appropriate way to happiness as voluptuous care and it has the structure of a virtue. Recall the account of happiness from Chapter 5. When, through our actions and attention, we succeed in making the good that is available to us persistently visible in our lives, we are justified in asserting our happiness. Happiness as voluptuous care requires a disposition to care because the things that matter to us are vulnerable and thus depend on our support. Sometimes, to sustain our connection to them, they require extraordinary support. We require a variety of relationships to simply survive and be healthy and many more relationships to lead a rich and full live. None of these relationships can survive without our disposition to care for the relationship as well as the people with whom we are related.

Equally important is the fact that care is one way we learn about what has value. Caring begins with a commitment to making the person cared for valuable. Care involves a kind of submission to the object in which the object of care reveals itself in a very particular way. We discover the genuine worth of things we value through the process of caring for them. Involvement is a process of discovery.

Caring allows us to recognize and understand the particularity and individuality of the person cared for, information that is not available through disinterested involvement or by relying on stereotypes.

To claim that care has the structure of a virtue is to say that care must be learned. It is not a spontaneous, untutored reaction to things in the environment but is a complex set of motivations and capacities that one acquires through a process of trial and error. Like Aristotle's virtues, it can be understood as a mean between two extremes. Care can be performed too much or too little, can be performed at the right time or the wrong time, and can be directed towards appropriate or inappropriate objects. If I care for one person when someone else needs more attention, or support projects that lack value, or care in intrusive ways, I am missing the mean; the failure is a vice.

This version of the ethics of care understands care to be dominant virtue. That is to say that other virtues are virtues because they contribute to our caring responses. Courage, for instance, is a virtue because it enables us to defend that which is vulnerable. Loyalty helps us sustain our connections to people about which we care; honesty sustains the trust needed to preserve relationships. Justice is required to strike the proper balance between things we care about, so that each receives the care it deserves.

However, care cannot be the only dominant virtue for reasons suggested by the following examples. Suppose a very close friend, whom I have known for a long time and care deeply about, announces to me in strict confidence that he is about to commit a crime – an act of environmental terrorism. The crime is in the service of a worthy cause – environmental protection – to which he and I have been committed for a long time. However, the act will involve some destruction of property and may put people at risk, although there is no intent to harm people and steps will be taken to avoid harming them. My friend is convinced of the moral worth of his act, but I am not – in fact, I am convinced that such violent acts are morally wrong and strategically questionable.

For an analysis of the ethics of care, this situation raises the question of whether a caring person is required to endorse or support the goals of the person cared for when those goals may be wrong or without value. Intuitively, it would seem wrong to demand of someone that they support goals they feel unworthy regardless of the nature of the relationship. Or consider a quite different case that raises similar issues. Suppose that your mother, as she gets older, increasingly becomes critical of the way you live your life and is disappointed with the amount of attention she receives from you, though you call or visit regularly. Many of her comments are insulting and hurtful, and apparently intended to be so. She desperately needs your companionship and support but she engages in various forms of emotional blackmail in order to secure it. Her behaviour makes the time you spend together both unpleasant and demeaning, causing you to become mean-spirited and cynical as well and harming relationships with your own family. In short, the relationship is becoming destructive. You have spoken to her about this and even suggested psychological counselling, but she simply takes that as more evidence of your lack of concern.

Here the issue is whether there are limits to care and how we should justify those limits. Intuitively, it seems as though there must be some limits. In order for a person to be caring, we cannot require that she preserve all relationships even to the point of destroying other aspects of life. These examples suggest that care as a dominant virtue sometimes conflicts with another dominant virtue – moral integrity. We must be concerned with our own character as much as we are concerned with the welfare of others. Therefore, it is more accurate to refer to care as a co-dominant virtue.

INTEGRITY

Integrity refers to the extent to which our various commitments form a harmonious, intact whole. One of the more accessible ways of describing integrity is to appeal to the structure of the self discussed in Chapter 1. Recall that according to Frankfurt, the self is arranged in hierarchical fashion. We have desires for various goods (first-order desires), and also desires that we have certain desires. (second-order desires, values, etc.). There can be third- and fourth-order desires or values as well. According to Frankfurt, to have integrity is to bring these various levels of desire into harmony and wholeheartedly identify with them so that one's actions are consistent with them.

I will suggest modifications in this account of integrity below, but for now we can think of integrity as involving two kinds of coherence. First, there must be coherence between one's commitments, principles or values. A person would lack integrity if she had many conflicting desires and always acted on her strongest desire at each moment with no deliberation about which desires are worthwhile. She would be a house divided, her actions lacking the constancy that is required to find value in things. Second, there must be coherence between a person's actions and her desires, values and commitments. A person lacks integrity if she acts contrary to her highest-order commitments or values because she would not be true to herself, acting in opposition to what is important to her.

Self-knowledge is essential for integrity because we have to know what our values and commitments are if we are to put them in order. Integrity requires that we discriminate between first-order desires using our higher-order system of values to rule them out or endorse them. For instance, you may endorse a desire to study and rule out a desire to go to the movies tonight because achievement in school is a higher-order value than watching car chases and digitally-enhanced explosions. However, there can be conflicts between higher-order values. Achievement in school isn't everything and you might value time spent with friends as a higher-order value as well. Thus, if your friends want to go to the movie, you might still be drawn to attending the movie, despite your desire to do well in school. This conflict can be resolved either by endorsing one of the desires in conflict or by appealing to an even higher-order value – perhaps you have resolved in general to be less distracted by the temptations of ordinary life. Persons who are able to resolve such conflicts without continuing to feel deeply torn between the values in play have integrity; persons who cannot do not have integrity.

Desires, commitments and values are of course constantly changing, so integrity is not something one simply has, but instead requires a continual process of renewal and adaptation. This account of integrity requires that a person of integrity has some things that they must do or must not do in order to continue to be the person one is. There must be some commitments that are unconditional in that to violate them would be to lose the sense that one has a stable sense of self. These commitments I referred to as identity-conferring commitments in earlier chapters and are to be distinguished from things we are committed to but could lose without feeling remorse. For instance, if a soldier claims that his highest commitment is to be loyal to his country, his military unit and the success of his mission, and defines himself according to those commitments, but then cuts and runs at the first sign of enemy fire, he can no longer claim to have those unconditional commitments – he is not the person he thought he was.

By contrast, a person who loves metal-rap but after a while grows tired of guitar riffs did not have an identity-conferring commitment – just a preference that was not sufficiently embedded in his psychology to count as identity-conferring.

Why is integrity a virtue? It satisfies the requirements of being a disposition that must be learned through practice. Integrity is not easy to sustain because of the competing demands on our time and resources. Knowing how to make small adjustments in our commitments that enable us to sustain the value of what we care about requires a good deal of trial and error. Moreover, integrity is the sort of thing we need in the right amount, at the right time, and for the right reason. We can have too much integrity and be inflexible and unresponsive, or we can have too little integrity and be fickle and irresolute. I will say more about this below.

But more importantly, integrity is required by the conception of happiness as voluptuous care. As we saw in the previous chapter, identity-conferring commitments are central to happiness because happiness requires that we persistently find value in our lives over the long haul. Identity-conferring commitments help us do that because they are stable elements in our psychologies that we cannot sacrifice without suffering psychological trauma.

Integrity plays an important role in regulating the virtue of care. Recall that the problem with care as a dominant virtue is that it can be unreasonably demanding, directed towards the wrong objects, or require us to violate other moral requirements. Because integrity is a co-dominant virtue as well, it prevents a virtuous person from allowing the demands of care from overwhelming other values including the importance of self-respect, personal autonomy, etc. A person of integrity acknowledges the various commitments she has and the variety of things and activities that are important and strives to find coherence among them, without allowing any of them to be seriously compromised. Thus, in caring for my friend, I need not endorse his environmental terrorism; in caring for your mother you need not subject yourself to her demeaning attacks if doing so would seriously compromise some other commitment. Thus, an ethic of care, when coupled with the virtue of integrity, is not subject to the complaint that it fails the livability criterion, a potential criticism raised in Chapter 3.

However, there are two problems with integrity as a moral ideal. One is that unconditional commitments can be based on almost anything. A person deeply devoted to his skill as an assassin might have integrity since his commitments may be consistent and his actions in conformity with them. In ordinary discourse we often speak of a person of integrity as someone who is honest or fair. But this discourse doesn't reflect the nature of integrity, but rather the contexts in which we typcially choose to apply the term. By itself, integrity refers to the coherence of a viewpoint, not its content.

However, the neutrality of integrity regarding moral actions is not a problem if integrity is not the only dominant virtue. Because care is a co-dominant virtue, care and relationship obligations provide moral content to the idea of integrity. Thus, the first problem is manageable.

However, a second, deeper problem with integrity points towards an obstacle that virtue ethics in general must overcome. Happiness, as I have described it, requires a pluralist conception of value. There are many things of value that we can enjoy. Care and integrity help us to enjoy them fully and are a component in that enjoyment. But values, obligations, commitments and virtues are inherently diverse and probably cannot be reconciled into a harmonious system that eliminates conflict. Conflict between goods can exist at many levels – between cultures, groups within a culture, between persons – but here we focus on conflicts within a person. For example, identity-conferring commitments can come into conflict, as when a talented musician's commitment to her art conflicts with her desire to spend more time with her children. Virtues can conflict as well. Integrity – coherence in one's basic commitments – can conflict with a desire to be more responsive to new demands on one's capacity to care, as when a family member's health crisis demands so much of your time and attention that you can no longer maintain a sense that your life forms an intelligible whole. The virtue of honesty might demand that I tell a difficult truth to someone, while the virtue of kindness might suggest that I tell a lie to avoid causing them pain.

Given such conflict, how can we achieve the wholeheartedness and coherence that constitutes integrity? In fact, the existence of conflict threatens the role that integrity plays in the achievement of happiness. Imagine a fully integrated person whose first-order desires are regulated by second-order desires that she wholeheartedly endorses and whose actions conform rigorously to her values. Such a person may not be able to experience the pull of new, perhaps fugitive desires that may not fit within her system of values. Such a limitation may prevent a person from enjoying what has value in her context.

Furthermore, if we are excessively concerned with resolving conflicts between commitments, we may tend to avoid genuine sources of value. It may take too much effort to care about the many things that have value if our commitments tear us apart. Thus, the pursuit of integrity ought to encourage me to limit the persons and activities to which I am committed. Too much integrity inhibits the pursuit of happiness. Both Aristotle's conception of virtue and Frankfurt's conception of integrity assume that a good person acts on the basis of a unified vision of a good life. Although Aristotle expresses a degree of admiration for people who do the right thing but struggle to deal with conflicting desires, he argues that a virtuous person does not have such conflicts. Similarly, Frankfurt's notion of wholeheartedness suggests an absence of conflict is desirable once a decision has been made to act.

Unfortunately, I doubt that in contemporary society with our diverse commitments and pressures, anyone can be open to the enjoyment of what has value and manage to live without conflicts. Wholeheartedness seems out of the question. Nevertheless, we can experience conflicts of values and emotions without losing the motivation to act. Virtues are necessary because without them, the things we care about are vulnerable. To cancel the value of things in order to achieve peace of mind leads us away from virtue not towards it. To be virtuous is to proceed in full knowledge of what is at risk. Integrity thus requires the virtue of courage. To have integrity we have to bear some losses without flinching.

Once again, emotions play an essential role in explaining what it means to maintain integrity in the face of conflict. Martha Nussbaum argues that a virtuous person not only acts appropriately; she experiences the appropriate feelings as well. She argues that when we confront tragic circumstances in which choosing one moral response will inevitably cause harm to something else we care about, there may be no resolution no matter how imaginative we are. In such cases, a good person can preserve her moral integrity by expressing the appropriate emotion that sustains her commitment to the compromised values. To express genuine remorse at having broken a promise to one's child in order to keep a promise to another is to indicate that the disappointed child is still valued. This emotional response preserves our integrity since it indicates that the agent remains steadfast in her commitment to the compromised value

In dealing with this issue of conflicts between identity-conferring commitments, we make a mistake if we think of integrity as static or unchanging. Identity-conferring commitments, in part, make us who we are. But as selves each of us is constantly changing. What matters is that despite these changes we remain intelligible to ourselves and others – that there is enough continuity to the self that we can be held responsible over time for our actions.

The precise nature of this continuity has long been a topic of great debate among philosophers, a debate we cannot rehearse in detail here. But for our purposes in articulating the kind of continuity that moral integrity requires, it is helpful to think of self-identity as a kind of narrative. Paul Ricoeur, Alasdair MacIntyre and Nina Rosenstand have argued that human beings view themselves as continuous through the many changes in a lifetime by representing themselves in a narrative. We grasp our own experience and the experience of others as interconnected stories with beginnings, midpoints and anticipated endings. The way we anticipate the endings of our narrative give structure to experience because they give significance to past and present.

Identity is the product of an extended thought process in which individuals go over their lives and edit them in light of their present circumstances and expectations for the future in a way that enables them to continually move towards that future. Our lives make sense if we can tell a coherent story about where we have been, where we are and where we are going. The stories we tell about ourselves involve a series of constant adjustments of our understanding of our past and present in light of our future – the self is being constantly reinterpreted. By contrast, if, in making decisions and judgements, we simply leap from one incongruous choice to another without linking our decisions to attachments from the past and plans for the future regarding how we achieve happiness, we will lead fragmented lives with little connection to what matters. Identity-conferring commitments are a significant element in the unity of these narratives – they represent common threads that link the various narrative episodes in our lives. To have integrity, then, is to be capable of living an integrated narrative – the story has unity because the various identity-conferring commitments co-exist in relatively stable relationships. However, narrative unity is not a matter of all elements being simultaneously in some kind of balanced equilibrium. Tension, conflict and the persistence of a variety of loose ends in various degrees of resolution characterize the very best narratives. The stability and unity of a narrative unfolds over time.

Having integrity, then, is not a matter of integrating all commitments simultaneously, but rather of being able to make sense of our identities as they fluctuate over time. We cannot hold fast to all commitments at the same time, but we can often retrieve tomorrow what we put at risk today. We construct our identities out of materials that are unformed at any particular time, because the endings to the various plot lines of our stories still lie in the future. All action is carried out in light of my pursuit of voluptuous care, which is constantly shaping and reshaping my commitments, retrieving in them what looks valuable from the standpoint of an advancing narrative. Identity-conferring commitments must be constantly re-evaluated in light of new situations. Their power to confer identity on us arises precisely because they hold up under continual reassessment.

For instance, family commitments are important because they provide us with a sense of who we are despite the trials, separations, tragedies and traumas of life. But, of course, the sense of identity that family commitments gives us changes as we go through life. Family life, at least for many people, can be so rich with meaning that it can support multiple reinterpretations. Family life has one set of meanings for a child, another for an adolescent, still another for an elderly person. It means one thing for someone settled in her hometown, another for that same person who becomes a world traveller. When conflict arises, family commitments will withstand some degree of compromise because they are the sort of thing that has that depth of meaning. By contrast, a commitment that cannot be reinterpreted to accommodate development may be one not worth maintaining.

On this view, having integrity means that when we make a decision to reassess a commitment, the fact that it figures prominently in our narrative self-conception counts heavily in its favour. We take higher-order values more seriously than first-order desires and resist reassessment of those values, unless the narrative unity of our lives requires reassessment. Integrity, on this view, does not require the absence of conflict; since conflict is integral to the idea of a narrative. Rather, integrity requires that agents focus on developing their narratives in ways that potentially resolve conflict, that produce cogent and coherent re-descriptions of commitments when the developing narrative of one's life requires new resources. Like identity, integrity is not something we simply have, but something we have to struggle to maintain.

PRACTICAL WISDOM

The inevitability of conflict and the demands of integrity point out the need for one more codominant virtue – practical wisdom. The virtues we have discussed thus far have been virtues of character. They are dispositions to live well that are acquired through training and habitual activity that enable us to do the right thing at the right time and in the right way. But in order to acquire the character virtues we must make difficult judgements about what is most important in a situation, and these judgements must be guided by an understanding of what has genuine value. In other words, there is an intellectual component to living well, which we call practical wisdom. Aristotle included this in his list of intellectual virtues and argued that it plays an essential role in the development of a moral virtue. None of the character virtues can be acquired without practical wisdom. Thus, it is not just one virtue among others but a kind of executive virtue that makes the others possible.

Practical wisdom is deliberation about living a good life, and is especially concerned with getting the many aspects of a good life to fit together in a coherent whole. Practical wisdom enables us to answer the question: 'How can we advance goals and act on commitments that must be revisable given that we must pursue a variety of conflicting goods?'

Thus, a central component of practical wisdom is the ability to be sensitive to the requirements of particular circumstances and the ability to modify our ends to accommodate all of what we care about. It is practical wisdom that enables us to know when generosity is appropriate given limited resources, to know when to show gratitude while not seeming obsequious, to know when interference in a person's life might do more harm than good. As I noted above in the discussion of care, this ability requires emotional connection and sensitivity as well as a cognitive grasp of moral concepts and a reflective understanding of one's own experience.

Practical wisdom may involve some understanding of moral rules and principles, as ways of summing up past experience. But these rules do not replace the requirement that action is guided by context-sensitive judgement. So to have practical wisdom one must know what things are worth caring about, the appropriate ways of caring about them, and the actions that we perform at the right time and in the right way to preserve that about which we care.

What are the components of practical wisdom? Aristotle's doctrine of the mean is a helpful starting point for thinking about this because the capacity to shape emotions in order to appropriately respond to the world is essential to living well. Aristotle's doctrine of the mean entails that self-control is part of practical wisdom. A wise person not only knows what is to be done but can use that understanding to shape her impulses, so that her actions conform to her understanding. However, although helpful, Aristotle's account does not unpack the variety of other skills that make up this capacity. Moreover, the doctrine of the mean, because it seeks moderation, seems incompatible with strong passions and the kinds of excesses that often give rise to creativity. Yet, creativity is an essential component of happiness as voluptuous care. Thus, we need a more expansive understanding of practical wisdom than Aristotle provides.

What follows is a thumbnail sketch of at least some of the capacities involved in practical wisdom.

(1) Reasoning ability

To act well an agent must know what the purpose or end result of an action is, know why that end result is desirable, develop a strategy for achieving that end result, judge the effectiveness of competing strategies, and make a decision to carry out one of those strategies. Thus, practical wisdom requires all of the skills we normally associate with intelligence: the ability to make logical inferences, to synthesize and interpret information, recognize similarities and differences, etc.

(2) Knowledge of how the world works

For an agent to make judgements about what is worth caring about and develop strategies for sustaining caring relationships, she has to know a great deal about human needs, how those needs are embedded in the natural world in which we live, the most effective ways of satisfying those needs, and how to use this information to make accurate predictions. Thus, general knowledge of nature, human nature and psychology is essential. A broad understanding of history, social science and natural science is necessary in order to make informed judgements about how to cope with human vulnerability.

These capacities refer to our general ability to diagnose and solve problems. But practical wisdom requires that we solve problems in ways that preserve moral integrity. Moreover, before we can reason about problems that arise, before we know what generalizations about human nature are appropriate, we have to get an accurate vision of what our situation is. Thus, moral wisdom goes beyond general intelligence to incorporate the following capacities.

(3) Moral attention and perception

Moral perception is the capacity to construe one's situation appropriately, to be responsive to the details of one's situation without the distraction of illusions or self-deception. This is an important skill because it provides the basis for subsequent deliberation, judgement and action. We will not deliberate about what action to take until we see the need for action. Thus, moral perception involves identifying a moral need and being sensitive to what is morally relevant in a situation, which may include various subtle features that are difficult to articulate. The word 'perception' here is in part metaphorical. Identifying morally relevant features of a situation is not a matter of pure sensory experience like observing a patch of colour. Rather, it involves a kind of intuitive understanding through which one grasps, in both a detailed and synthetic manner, the various factors that one must attend to in a situation in order to be morally responsible.

Phenomenologist Hubert Dreyfus has likened the capacity for excellent moral perception to a game of 'fast chess' played by experts who, despite the requirement to make a move in 5–10 seconds, can play with very little degradation in the quality of their game. His point is not that we should make ethical decisions quickly. Rather, he is claiming that expertise, in chess and morality, involves the use of finely trained intuitions rather than a process of analysis and deliberate comparison of alternatives.

The reason for this is that our relationships are not relationships with abstract characters but with real people who are distinctive and unique, and we can take them into moral consideration only if we embrace this distinctiveness. A friend is not just an occupant of a particular social role so that by exhaustively describing what it means to be a friend in general we have discovered all the morally relevant features of our interactions with friends. Drug addiction is a bad thing and not conducive to genuine friendship, but if my friend has become an addict, the morally relevant features of our situation will include subtle details of our shared histories and ways of framing the future that may apply only to us. Judgements about how much patience I should show, when to confront him and when to lay low, when to permit his self-deception and when to be honest, etc., are crucial to right action. Yet, nothing outside the particulars of our relationship determines what is right.

The situations we confront daily are embedded in social customs and personal and relational histories directed towards rival, incompatible values. Even a basic judgement such as whether something counts as a lie issues from a complex set of attitudes developed over the course of a unique individual's lifetime of social interaction. Thus, the upshot of moral perceptiveness will not be uniform across persons, even when they face similar circumstances. Rules or principles cannot function as reliable guides here. This is not to say that we never use principles. People in the process of acquiring moral expertise will, like chess players, learn the standard rules and strategic moves of their community and develop increasingly sophisticated ways of applying those rules in context. But genuine expertise will recognize rules as rough summaries of what seems to work most of the time and will develop more and more refined perceptions to guide actions.

Of course, as Dreyfus points out, when confronted with a situation so unfamiliar that we have no background of intuitive responses to rely on, we will have to fall back on principles, though our responses are likely to be crude and imprecise without the refinement that experience brings.

Moral perception requires moral attention as well. Because our situations are complex and new factors to consider are continually popping up, deliberation is often essential. As I noted above, even agents with good character will experience a variety of conflicting tugs in deciding what to do, and it takes time and effort to sort through them. Despite Dreyfus's comparison with 'fast chess', moral perception often involves effort and the patience to await clarity in a dynamic environment with many conflicting agendas. Thus, sustained attentiveness to things of value continuously builds complex attitudes and patterns of response that enable us to avoid indifference and respond to the claims of others.

British philosopher and novelist Iris Murdoch gives a wonderfully instructive account of moral attention. A mother, who Murdoch refers to as M, is hostile to her daughter-in-law D because she acts immaturely, has a bit of an accent in her speech, and is unpolished. In Britain's class-conscious society of the mid-twentieth century, M views her son as having married beneath his station – he could have done better. But as time goes on, M criticizes herself for leaping to such a judgement and with what Murdoch calls 'careful and just attention' gradually alters her view of D. She begins to see D, not as unpolished and immature, but as spontaneous, uncomplicated and full of youthful exuberance. Rather than being dismissive or contemptuous, M stays focused on D, and sustains with some struggle and frustration a position of care towards her that provides new insight into D's nature. In sustaining moral attention, M has perhaps changed her attitudes towards class differences as well.

Murdoch views this process as a matter of the ego getting out of the way enabling M to view her daughter-in-law impartially. But I think it is more appropriately viewed as a matter of recognizing the value in one's context. In admiring the youthful exuberance of her daughter-in-law, M has significantly advanced her own happiness by sustaining a relationship with a family member who is now a source of delight.

Before investigating additional components of practical wisdom, we need to address an objection to moral perception. Philosophers often treat appeals to moral perceptions with suspicion because they are not widely shared. My perceptions about a particular case will likely differ from yours even if we both have a wide range of experience. Thus, how can we be sure that our intuitions are not just arbitrary, subjective judgements that exhibit nothing but moral arrogance?

This criticism seems especially apt given my reliance on relationships as the foundation of ethics. Strong attachments often prevent us from seeing things clearly. The intensity of our concern with intimates can blind us to the pain of strangers, patriotism can blind us to the effects of war, etc. Even if the above account of moral perception is the correct description of how people with moral wisdom deliberate, we cannot conclude that the outcome of moral perception is justified. Intuitive or perceptual judgements are not correct because they are intuitive – they are correct because they are supported by good reasons. We need some way of distinguishing sound intuitive judgements from those based on ignorance or prejudice, and the best way to mark such a distinction is to see if the intuitions are based on sound theoretical principles.

This criticism is exactly right as a way of leading into a philosophical discussion of moral intuitions. As philosophers, we wish to hold ordinary judgements up to philosophical scrutiny and that is certainly a worthy enterprise. But our task is to understand practical wisdom, not philosophical method, and this criticism misses the mark in that regard. To see why, I want to introduce another feature of practical wisdom.

(4) Capacity for self-reflection

Even someone with a great deal of moral experience, perhaps especially people with a great deal of experience, may be set in their ways having formed a variety of habits they no longer reflect on. Any moral perception or intuition must be subject to correction and revision. We often confront situations in which our moral intuitions are questioned or criticized, fail to produce agreement, or have produced consequences we regret or did not intend. In such a situation, simply insisting on the rightness of our moral perceptions will not suffice, since they may have been arbitrary, biased, or ill-informed, or simply the result of habits not appropriate in the context. We have to gain a better understanding of the situation if we are to meet the challenge of disagreement or succeed in righting wrongs. However, the first line of defence against arbitrary, subjective judgements is not to try to find an impartial philosophical principle to help resolve the disagreement or clarify the situation. Rather a person of practical wisdom will engage in self-reflection.

Given that our perceptions are the product of many experiences built up over time, we first should entertain the possibility that our current understanding rests on a mistake. Dreyfus suggests that a wise person would typically try to re-experience the chain of events that led us to see things as we do, focusing on elements we may have missed in the past. We might imagine M thinking back to earlier instances when she may have misjudged someone because of superficial mannerisms. Dialogue with those who disagree may produce new insights into other ways of conceptualizing the situation, especially if they can articulate the process that led them to see the situation as they do. The motivation for such self-reflection, which can often be painful and difficult, is simply the desire for relationship and the recognition of its importance to our flourishing.

In any case, this process will not usually be a process of logical deduction from basic, impartial principles but a matter of soaking in the details of one's circumstances until something new presents itself. Of course, there is no guarantee of success. In the end, we may not be able to reach agreement or satisfy critics and our ordinary resources for self-reflection and dialogue may be insufficient in rooting out unwarranted prejudices that may be so deep that we can glimpse them only by adopting an impartial, theoretical view of our own beliefs. But as I have indicated, it is impossible to live in accordance with a belief and be utterly impartial at the same time. We are at the limits of practical wisdom here, because if we cannot find the impetus for change of view within our own experience or in our capacity to empathize with the experience of others it is not obvious how change of view can occur. We block our tendencies toward self-interested biases, not by being impartial, but by enabling a variety of attachments and commitments, sustained by moral attention, to guide our judgements. Practical imagination provides further resources for encouraging both a more expansive understanding of our own experience and a wide swathe of the experiences of others.

(5) Practical imagination

By practical imagination, I mean the ability to take all the relevant details of one's situation and imagine concretely how they can be transformed to produce a more acceptable future. We express ethical judgements in 'ought' statements – judgements about how the world ought to be. Ethics is centred on wanting something other than what exists, and thus always makes reference to a possible future. Thus, moral prescriptions inevitably take place as if we are mentally rehearsing a play. We judge our actions right or wrong by imagining what the future will be like if we choose one action rather than another. If I am deliberating about whether to keep a promise or not, I imagine, not only what the world will be like if I keep it or not, but what the world will be like given various ways of keeping or breaking promises.

The richer and more detailed our imaginings, the more finely tuned towards contextual complexities our actions will be if our imaginings are rooted in accurate moral perceptions. I call this 'practical imagination' because I am not referring to daydreaming or entertaining elaborate fictions. Practical imagination is an extension of our moral perceptions that accurately describe how things stand. Far from engaging in fantasy, practical imagination is directed towards actions that must bring about a plausible state of affairs in a context of substantial uncertainty. Even in the most serious of contexts, when we must have our feet firmly on the ground, we use imagination to help discover what to do.

Imagination plays another important role as well – it is essential to empathy and thus essential in coming to understand the full moral dimension of our situation. Often, our capacity to imaginatively dwell on the condition of other people will help us to understand their needs and the effects of our actions on them. Practical imagination sustains and holds open the fundamental desire for the world to be other than it is, a desire that is at the heart of ethics. Our shared vulnerability that contributes to the value things have draws us together and discloses a shared world of possibilities, but only if the imagination keeps us open to these possibilities. Maintaining openness to the world and its possibilities is a crucial dimension of ethics. Indifference and inattention is in part a failure of imagination.

In order to sustain imagination we have to immerse ourselves in as much difference as possible – alternative cultures, etc. We cannot draw on our own resources alone for imagination – it too requires relationship. A person of practical wisdom cannot be narrow, uninspired or excessively orthodox in her ability to conceptualize problem solutions.

The role of imagination in practical wisdom enables us to cope with one of the central problems in achieving and sustaining moral integrity. Remember, I argued above that to have moral integrity is to act in a reasonably wholehearted way in accordance with one's deepest values and commitments. However, our deepest commitments often come into conflict, and we often cannot act on one commitment without sacrificing something else that matters just as much, thus suffering a loss of integrity. When we successfully resolve such conflict, it is because we are able to imagine alternative possibilities that enable us to sustain commitments to everything about which we care.

When dealing with conflicts between work and family, competing obligations, or relationships that impose incompatible demands on us, the ability to view the conflict as an opportunity to find new ways of caring is essential. When work and family conflict we sometimes can discover novel work arrangements or a new career opportunities to avoid the conflict. When friends impose incompatible demands on us, finding a new way of understanding friendship (and the ability to convincingly articulate it) can mitigate the conflict.

However, it is often the case that we cannot resolve conflict. Ethics is a domain in which sometimes there simply are no solutions to problems. This simply follows from the idea that at least some values are incompatible. Yet, a person of character must cope with such situations. She does so through emotional intelligence.

(6) Emotional intelligence

When we are confronted by tragic choices that have no resolution, the best we can do is preserve the value of the option not acted on by showing the appropriate emotion. Emotions are necessary if we are to exercise moral perception, self-reflection and imagination. As I noted above in the discussion of care, emotional responses contribute to our moral perceptions by guiding us through the practical reasoning process. Empathy, compassion, shame, anger, guilt and more subtle affects such as vague feelings of trust or mistrust, anxiety, etc., sharpen our sense of what is morally relevant. They are also powerful motives that goad us into self-reflection and the process of imagining alternative futures.

QUALITIES OF CHARACTER AND MORAL REASONS

In Chapter 3, we developed a conception of moral reasoning that views moral reasons as organic products of relationships and consists primarily of picking out the appropriate moral property in a situation that requires our attention and response. But we left Chapter 3 with a variety of problems unresolved. We have made progress on some of these problems in subsequent chapters. We are now in a position to finally put them to rest.

If moral reasoning is about identifying morally relevant properties, how do we assess the relative strength of moral properties? Certain moral properties will stand out because they are the sort of thing a morally virtuous person attends to given a particular conception of what has value. Others will matter because they are required by the relationships in which we are embedded. Aristotle's doctrine of the mean, the epistemic role of emotions, the disposition to sustain relationships with care, the capacity to recognize the immediacy of need against a background of human vulnerability, and the demand to sustain personal integrity by employing practical reason, all constrain the kinds of reasons that will be justified in a particular set of circumstances.

Ultimately, a correct judgement is what a fully developed virtuous person judges to be correct in the appropriate context. Right action is a product of the exercise of specific virtues and thinking about what a virtue requires in a specific context determines the content of morality. This is the standard of correctness that governs all moral judgements. And this standard is itself justified because virtues are necessary to sustain and are a constituent part of the relationships that contribute to happiness as voluptuous care.

In closing, I want to take up one final issue that has percolated throughout this text. Perhaps the most serious potential objection to the argument of this book is that I have provided no resources for preventing the introduction of biases and prejudices into the reasoning process. I have argued that if 'impartial' means independent of our particular conceptions of what we care about then impartiality is simply not available to us. However, impartiality in a much more practical sense, means to become aware of how biases may enter our judgements and as much as possible try to eliminate them. We do this by exercising the virtues of care, integrity and practical wisdom – caring for the interests of others, considering points of view that conflict with our own, engaging in self-reflection and self-criticism when others object to our actions and judgements, and approaching differences with as much empathy and imagination as possible. Impartiality, like the other aspects of our moral lives, is in part a product of the kinds of relationships we develop. Deliberation is, at least to some degree, a collaborative process in which agent's clarify their point of view and expand their horizons only by remaining open to the perspective of others. These collaborative capacities do not guarantee the kind of impartiality that Kant and the utilitarians seek. But it is the only form of impartiality available to fallible human beings.

A FINAL WORD ABOUT OSKAR SCHINDLER

Given an understanding of qualities of moral character, we can finally grasp the motivations that might explain the actions of Schindler. Schindler was chosen for an extraordinary task. He found himself responsible for the lives of many people who had no other recourse than to rely on him. A person who possesses the virtues of care and integrity cannot easily discard a responsibility of such magnitude. For such a person in such a situation, the question is not 'Should I accept this burden or not?' because the burden has already been imposed. The question is 'Am I up to the task?' This question would crush most of us. Schindler was extraordinary because he saw opportunity in it.

We can do little but speculate about the factors that encouraged him to take up the task of rescuing his workers. However, we know that he was a charming, persuasive, opportunistic manipulator with the self-confidence to pull off this massive charade under the noses of brutal and suspicious guards. It may be the case that Schindler had built his life and his self-respect around his cunning, resourcefulness and willingness to take risks. Perhaps, as someone with integrity, he could not bear the thought of failing in these capacities. At any rate, we can see how the virtues of care, integrity and practical wisdom explain our capacity to be full moral agents.

REFERENCES AND SUGGESTIONS FOR FURTHER READING

Aristotle (1985), *The Nicomachean Ethics*, trans. Terence Irwin, Oxford: Oxford University Press.

Blum, Lawrence (1994), *Moral Perception and Particularity*, New York: Cambridge University Press.

Dreyfus, Hubert L. and Dreyfus, Stuart E. (1990), 'What is morality?: a phenomenological account of the development of ethical expertise', in David Rasmussen (ed.), *Universalism vs. Communitarianism*, Cambridge: MIT Press.

Frankfurt, Harry G. (1987), 'Identification and Wholeheartedness', in *Responsibility, Character and the Emotions*, ed. F. Schoeman, Cambridge: Cambridge University Press.

Furrow, Dwight (1998), 'Schindler's compulsion: an essay on practical necessity', in *American Philosophical Quarterly*. vol. 35, no. 3.

MacIntyre, Alasdair (1984), *After Virtue*, Indiana: University of Notre Dame Press.

Murdoch, Iris (1970), *The Sovereignty of the Good*, London/New York: Routledge.

Noddings, Nels (1984). *Caring: A Feminine Approach to Ethics and Moral Education*, Berkeley: University of California Press.
Nussbaum, Martha (1986), *The Fragility of Goodness*, Cambridge: Cambridge University Press.
Nussbaum, Martha (1990), *Love's Knowledge: Essays on Philosophy and Literature*, Oxford: Oxford University Press.
Ricoeur, Paul (1992), *Oneself as Another*, trans. Kathleen Blamey, Chicago: University of Chicago Press.
Rosenstand, Nina (2003), *The Moral of the Story*. (4th ed). New York: McGraw-Hill.

CHAPTER 7

MORAL RESPONSIBILITY

In Chapter 1, we saw that moral agency is dependent on our capacity to enter into and sustain relationships. This chapter continues that analysis by showing that assignments of moral responsibility are similarly dependent on relationships.

One of the most pervasive features of our social reality is the practice of praising or blaming people for their actions. Praise and blame are reactive attitudes as are resentment, anger, admiration, gratitude and indignation. They are reactions to something that someone has done. To view people (including oneself) as worthy of praise and blame is to ascribe moral responsibility to them. To say that someone is morally responsible for an action is to claim that they deserve praise or blame.

The concept of moral responsibility should not be confused with other uses of the word 'responsible'. We often speak of causal responsibility as in 'Yesterday's earthquake was responsible for the building's collapse.' The earthquake caused the collapse but was not morally responsible for it, because the earthquake did not intend the collapse. Earthquakes are not the sort of thing that can have intentions. As we will see shortly, causal responsibility is related to moral responsibility but is not identical to it since something can be causally responsible for an event without being morally responsible.

We also speak of people having certain responsibilities as the result of occupying a position or role, e.g. 'Police are responsible for public safety.' Role-responsibility differs from moral responsibility in that the responsibility is for something that ought to occur in the future. The police have a duty to make it the case that the public is safe. We often use the concept of responsibility when referring to the idea that a person is responsible because she has sufficient moral character to understand and take seriously moral requirements. Role responsibility (Chapter 4) and character responsibility (Chapter 6) have already been discussed under different headings. For a person to be responsible in either sense, they must be capable of assignments of moral praise and blame, so we will ignore these other uses of responsibility for now since the idea of moral responsibility is more basic.

THE PROBLEM OF FREE WILL

The concept of moral responsibility receives a lot of philosophical discussion because it seems to be central to our idea of a person. According to many philosophers, the main feature that distinguishes persons from earthquakes, animals and other natural processes is that only persons deserve praise and blame for at least some of their actions. To deserve moral praise and blame is what is distinctive about human beings.

The philosophical difficulty with this idea is that it is not obvious why human beings deserve praise or blame for what they do. The difficulty arises because assignments of moral responsibility seem to require that the person being praised or blamed chose to do what she did – that she acted freely. In other words, if I am morally responsible for failing to keep a promise to allow my daughter to have the car tonight, it must be the case that I could have kept the promise and chose not to. If I could not have kept my promise because, through no fault of mine, the car was defective, I cannot be blamed for it. I did not choose to violate my promise. To be responsible, my action must be a free action. And, according to many philosophers, to be a free action it must be the case that I could have done otherwise – I could have chosen differently.

This suggests that freedom of will is best defined as the ability to do otherwise. If you decided to go to the movies tonight instead of studying for your exam, your action – going to the movies – was a free action if and only if you could have chosen to do something else. But according to one very plausible account of how the world works, we cannot act freely. This position is called determinism; if determinism is true it threatens our assignments of moral responsibility. This is not the place to debate the issue of free will and determinism, but some discussion of this issue is required to understand the puzzle that moral responsibility poses.

Determinism is based on the simple claim that every event has a cause sufficient to bring that event about. Every event is caused by prior states of affairs along with the causal laws that explain how events are related. When my car did not start this morning, it was because the state of the engine just prior to my turning the key, and the laws that govern internal combustion engines, were such that the car did not start. Given the dead battery and all the other conditions at that time, there was no alternative to the car not starting. Its' not starting was determined.

This principle that every event has a cause is a common sense idea that we routinely accept about all events. Moreover, it is a basic principle of science at least for ordinary sized objects. Aside from isolated, quantum mechanical states, the physical universe appears to be deterministic. However, human beings are physical systems just as automobiles are and human behaviour follows laws every bit as deterministic as automobiles. When I decided to get a cup of coffee, that decision was caused by the state of my brain and nervous system just prior to my making the decision. Thus, at that point in time, given my psychology, I could not have done otherwise. If my brain state had been different, I could have decided on fruit juice rather than coffee, but given my psychology at that time, my action was determined. Every action is the product of complex bio-chemical reactions in the brain. Even when I deliberate about what to do, that deliberation is the product of these bio-chemical reactions and thus the outcome is determined. And all of my brain states are traceable to environmental and genetic causes, so at no point in my life could I ever have done otherwise than what I did.

Of course, we do not know everything there is to know about our brain states and what is influencing them, and we are far from knowing all the laws that govern brain states, so we cannot reliably predict what human beings will do. In that sense, we are quite unlike automobiles. But we could make such predictions if we had the knowledge. Thus, our actions are not free. The determinist will grant that our experience of free will is a basic element of human consciousness. But this experience is due to our brain's complexity and our lack of detailed knowledge. Our awareness of free will is not evidence of its existence.

If determinism is true, it obviously creates many problems for moral responsibility. If people cannot choose their actions, if they could not do other than what they did, it doesn't make much sense to praise or blame them for what they did. If determinism is true, it looks like our assignments of praise and blame and our reactive attitides are unjustified and indeed irrational.

Determinism is a controversial view and many philosophers (as well as most non-philosophers) reject it because it threatens our fundamental notions of personhood and moral responsibility. However, the alternative position – indeterminism – is fraught with problems that make it difficult to accept.

Indeterminists argue for the intuitively plausible claim that we have free will and thus are morally responsible for at least some of our actions. But this argument depends on either denying the basic principle of common sense and science that every event has a cause, or claiming that some actions are the product of reasons not causes. The first approach in effect argues that free actions are random events. But if this is the case the indeterminist has to explain how we are in control of our actions if they are random. It is important for the concept of moral responsibility that I am in control of actions for which I am responsible. But how can I be in control of an action if it is uncaused.

The second approach must claim that our capacity to reason cannot be reduced to a causal process. In other words, when I give reasons for my action I am not citing the causes of my action. Actions that are the product of reasons are free, whereas actions that are the product of causes are not. For instance, it is one thing to claim that my decision to have tofu for dinner was caused by my craving tofu. That is to give a causal explanation. But if I explain my decision to have tofu as a decision guided by reasoning about its nutrients and benefits to health, then I have given quite a different explanation – one that appeals to reason. To the extent my decision is guided by reasons it is free decision.

But this approach is problematic because the indeterminist must now explain why one set of reasons appeal to her more than others, and it is not obvious why the answer to this question is not traceable to bio-chemical reactions in the brain and nervous system, and ultimately to environmental and genetic causes.

Thus, with regard to the issue of moral responsibility we seem to be in a difficult situation. We must give up the plausible idea that we are morally responsible for some of our actions or give up the equally plausible idea that every event has a cause. Dissatisfaction with this dilemma has encouraged the development of a compromise position called soft determinism or compatibilism.

Compatibilists agree with the determinists that every event has a cause and prior conditions and physical laws determine all of our actions. However, compatibilists argue that determinism is compatible with freedom of the will – hence the designation 'compatibilism'. Compatibilists are able to make this compromise by redefining the idea of a free action. Recall that for both determinists and indeterminists an action is free if and only if the agent performing the action could have done otherwise. Compatibilists argue that this definition is misleading. To see why let's reconsider the decision to go to the movies or study for an exam. Suppose your friends are pleading with you to go to see *The Attack of the Killer Tomatoes*, a movie that you are dying to see. But you have a philosophy exam tomorrow that you have not studied for. So you deliberate about what matters to you. You really want to spend more time with your friends, you really will enjoy the movie, philosophy has gotten so tedious lately and you're not even sure you know why it matters. Thus, given who you are at that point in time – your system of desires, values, intentions, patterns of decision-making, etc. – you choose to go to the movies. According to the definition of a free action as the ability to do otherwise, that very same deliberative process, your psychological state at the point of decision, could have produced the alternative result – a decision to study for the exam. Compatibilists complain that someone who deliberates in this way would be utterly capricious and arbitrary. How could the same psychological state produce an alternative action unless the action was completely disconnected from a coherent and logical process of thought?

The compatibilist will argue that what matters to us is that our actions are the product of our characters, our actions express who we are at a particular point in time. The fact that our actions are determined by our characters doesn't make an action unfree. To the contrary, that is exactly what a free action is – an action I perform because I want to. So the compatibilist modifies the definition of freedom. An action is free if, and only if, the agent is doing what she wants. The ability to do otherwise does not matter to us; what matters to us is the ability to do what we want. As long as our actions are voluntary, with no external impediments, our actions are free. But this conception of freedom is compatible with determinism. When you chose to go to the movies rather than study, your action was determined by your psychological state (beliefs, desires, intentions) just prior to the action. And that psychological state was determined by prior psychological states, etc., eventually traceable to environmental and genetic influences. Thus, our actions are free yet determined.

The indeterminist will reject this compromise claiming that it matters to us how our characters and psychological states are formed. In order to be genuinely free we need some sort of control over our psychological states. Thus, they claim that the compatibilist's definition of freedom is impoverished.

Traditional conceptions of moral responsibility have typically rested on assumptions about whether indeterminism or compatibilism provide the best account of free will. Deontological theories of ethics typically have adopted a merit-based view of moral responsibility, which ultimately rests on indeterminism. An agent is responsible for an action if and only if she deserves praise or blame. And an agent deserves praise and blame for an action if and only if she could have done otherwise. Utilitarian theories of ethics have adopted a consequentialist view of moral responsibility, which ultimately rests on compatibilism. We should hold an agent responsible for an action, if and only if doing so would be overall beneficial, especially in producing improvement in the agent's behaviour. According to compatibilism, our actions are ultimately determined by environmental and genetic influences. If praise or blame will influence an agent's conduct in ways that produce good consequences, then assignments of praise and blame are justified.

The difficulty here is that the appropriateness of our practices of praising and blaming people for what they do, which are central features of our moral lives, rest on difficult and controversial metaphysical claims about free will and determinism which have not been and perhaps cannot be decisively validated. It would be of great benefit if we could come up with a coherent account of moral responsibility that does not rely on metaphysics for its justification.

MORAL RESPONSIBILITY WITHOUT METAPHYSICS

Happily, there is an alternative approach to the problem of moral responsibility that was developed by P.F. Strawson in 1962. Strawson argued that, in order to hold people responsible for their actions, we need not know how the action actually came about in the physical universe. What matters is that our attitudes towards the actions of other persons express what we care about in our relationships with them. The reactive attitudes of praise and blame are natural reactions to how others view us and how much their actions matter to us, given that both of us are participants in a particular relationship.

We expect others to act towards us with a reasonable degree of good will and when they do not we blame them for it. Agents deserve praise and blame depending on whether they have met our demands to be treated with respect or not. These judgements can be suspended or modified with regard to specific actions and events. If someone harms me by accident I do not blame her because the harm was not intended – it did not bear the marks of ill will. We can also suspend our judgements of praising and blaming when we judge that someone or something is incapable of participating in a full range of relationships and is thus outside the moral community. Some animals, very young children, the severely psychologically impaired and inanimate objects are not appropriate subjects for the reactive attitudes.

The reactive attitudes regulate first, second and third person responses. I can be angry at myself for something I have done, angry at someone else for what they have done to me, and angry at someone else for what she has done to others. Thus, for Strawson, the reactive attitudes express the interpersonal nature of human existence. To be a person is to exist with other persons and to be both capable of these reactive attitudes and a target of them as well. The concept of moral responsibility is wholly defined by these reactive attitudes and the way we use them. Thus, they are not based on any independent reasons outside the framework of human social life. They are simply part of our social nature and need no further justification. It is unlikely we could get rid of them in any case and neither would it be desirable to do so. Social life would be unintelligible without these attitudes. What makes them rational is not that they are grounded in the correct account of metaphysical freedom but that they are reflections of how social beings must interact if relationships are to be sustained.

Independently of whether human beings have free will, what matters is whether a person has the appropriate interpersonal attitudes as defined by our practices of holding people responsible. Of course, in particular cases, whether a person exhibits the appropriate attitudes or not can be a matter of uncertainty. But we resolve that uncertainty by focusing on what the agent's intentions were and what role they play in the relationship, not whether they had free will.

Strawson's view fits with the general theme of this book that we can best understand moral phenomena by focusing on relationships.

But Strawson is not without his critics. The main objection is that it commits us to irrationalism in an essential area of our lives since these attitudes can't be defended – they are just part of our nature that we must accept. It is excessively credulous to take moral and social practices at face value without criticism or evaluation. For instance, the fact that society chooses to hold adolescents in their early teens fully responsible for serious crimes they commit does not make that practice morally right. Obviously there are cases of holding people responsible which are unfair or cruel. This may be one of those cases. Thus, we need some standards through which we can assess our current practices of holding people responsible, and the issue that immediately comes to mind is whether they are sufficiently focused on the degree to which an agent is in control of their actions.

A second worry that some philosophers have with Strawson's view is that in some cases our reactive attitudes do seem to be regulated by the degree of freedom appropriately attributed to a person. For instance, if a person commits a crime while under the influence of very powerful drugs, it seems appropriate to say they are less responsible, not because they lack good will, but because they had diminished control over their action.

Strawson shows that we can make sense of the practice of assignments of moral responsibility without deciding the debate between determinism and indeterminism. What we need, to set aside these objections, is an account of when agents are in control of their actions that does not require a solution to the debate between determinism and indeterminism. Contemporary philosophers John Fischer and Mark Ravissa provide such an account that will help resolve some of these difficulties.

GUIDANCE CONTROL AND MORAL RESPONSIBILITY

Fischer and Ravissa argue that agents have control over their actions when they have the capacity to respond to reasons. They begin to spell out what it means to be responsive to reasons by distinguishing two kinds of control an agent might have over her actions – guidance control and regulative control. Guidance control means that agents have control over the actual sequence of events leading to an action. If I want bagels for breakfast, know where to get them, and this belief and desire cause me to get bagels for breakfast then I have guidance control. Regulative control involves both control over the actual sequence of events and the ability to do otherwise. In order to have regulative control, not only must my getting bagels result from my beliefs and desires, I also must have the ability to do otherwise, e.g. choose bacon and eggs.

Fischer and Ravissa illustrate these two forms of control by imagining the following cases. In the first case, imagine that Sally is driving her car and is capable of choosing a variety of routes to get to her destination. She chooses one route but could have chosen others. In the second case, a driving instructor is monitoring Sally's driving and has his own steering wheel that allows him to override her decisions. If she turns onto a route other than the one her instructor wants her to take, the instructor will override her decision. Sally, though, in deciding which route to take happens to drive along the route the instructor prefers and he never has to take control of the car. In both cases, Sally freely chooses the route she takes. But in the first case Sally has guidance control and regulative control. She directs the car down the route she wants (guidance control) *and* has the ability to do otherwise and drive down a different route (regulative control).

In the second case, however, Sally has guidance control since she drives the car down the route she wants. But she does not have regulative control because she cannot take an alternate route given the presence of the instructor's override ability. The second case shows that even if we do not have the ability to do otherwise, we nevertheless have an important kind of control over our actions – guidance control.

This is straightforward compatibilism, as I described it above. Guidance control means that our actions are being guided by what we want, by our character, values, etc. Sally is acting freely because she is doing what she wants. Fischer and Ravissa then argue that this is the relevant kind of control required for moral responsibility. To illustrate, let's extend Fischer and Ravissa's example. Suppose that Sally in choosing the route she wants intends to kill her husband, who is following in the car behind her, by activating a timed device that will set off a roadside bomb just as her husband passes. Suppose that her new boyfriend, the driving instructor, plans on insuring that Sally doesn't lose her courage and choose a different route by being prepared to override Sally's control of the car. Sally doesn't lose heart and drives down the road as planned, thereby activating the bomb killing her husband. Sally is morally responsible for her action, though she could not have done otherwise and therefore lacked regulative control. Sally's guidance control is sufficient to secure a judgement that she is morally responsible.

This argument does not demonstrate the truth of determinism, indeterminism or compatibilism. It simply shows that independently of that issue, we can find grounds for attributing moral responsibility to Sally. The question for us is why guidance control is sufficient for moral responsibility. According to Fischer and Ravissa, guidance control is based on the fact that human beings are responsive to reasons. If a person was induced to commit a crime through hypnosis, we would claim she is not morally responsible. The reason for this judgement would be that she cannot respond to reasons not to commit the crime. Telling her that she may be incarcerated or that the act is wrong would have no effect because her psychological state is such that she cannot entertain reasons. Such a person lacks guidance control over her behaviour. When we assign moral responsibility to people, we assume that if they were given sufficient reason for not doing the action then they would refrain from doing it. The fact that they would respond to reasons indicates that they are in control of their actions and are thus responsible.

What about Sally when she kills her husband? Is she responsive to reasons? At first it might not appear that she is. If she had thought of a reason not to kill her husband, she still could not have avoided the murder because her boyfriend would override her decision. But assuming she was not psychologically damaged in some way, she could have changed her mind, in which case the murder which she inevitably committed would have been against her will just as in the hypnosis case. The point here is that when assigning moral responsibility we look at the actual sequence of events that explain an action, and the mechanisms (i.e. Sally's capacity for practical reason) that are part of that sequence. If that mechanism is asserting guidance control by responding to reasons, then we are justified in assigning responsibility. We don't worry about whether alternative possibilities were available that are not part of the actual sequence. If Sally's brain is functioning well enough to respond to reasons, then Sally was acting freely and was responsible for her action regardless of her boyfriend's power to override her decisions.

The upshot of these examples is that to be morally responsible, I must have guidance control. To have guidance control is to be able to act from one's own beliefs and desires, just as Sally did, and to act from a mechanism (her capacity for deliberation) that is responsive to reason as presumably Sally's was. Fischer and Ravissa add additional conditions to their account of moral responsibility, but we can ignore them for our purposes. The important point is that their account of guidance control gives us a handle on how we can go about evaluating our social practices of praise and blame. We can evaluate our norms governing the assignment of praise and blame by testing them against a standard of guidance control.

However, I want to argue now that there are problems with this account of guidance control which suggest that it has application only within the broader framework of Strawson's view that attributions of moral responsibility are fundamentally judgements we make about the requirements and coherence of social relations. In some contexts, issues of control should take precedence. In other contexts, the requirements of social relations will take precedence, and no precise theoretical account of when one should take precedence over the other is available. To begin to discuss these problems, I want to return to the issue of reasons responsiveness.

Recall that an agent is in control if she is responsive to reasons and she is responsive to reasons if it is the case that if sufficient reasons were presented to her for acting otherwise, then at least in some cases she would act differently. But if a person acts as she does regardless of the reasons presented to her then she is not reasons responsive and not in control. The responsiveness to reasons condition is a bit tricky because it demands that we distinguish people who are capable of morality but fail to do what is right from people who are incapable of acting on moral reasons because of an incapacity. A person is responsible for wrongdoing if she was in general responsive to reason, but in some particular case failed to appropriately respond. By contrast, the insane or very young children cannot act on moral reasons at all and are thus not responsible. Someone who should act on a reason and fails to do so is responsible if she was capable of responding to reasons.

But there are endless complications in working out how responsive to reasons an agent must be in order to be morally responsible. If we had to be responsive to all objectively sufficient reasons, none of us would be responsible. Even the best of us are irrational some of the time, and often our reasoning is deployed in contexts where objectivity is inappropriate, e.g. when emotional connections and commitments are at stake. On the other hand, if a person only occasionally responds to reason, e.g. a drug addict who would refrain from shooting up only when her favourite song comes on the radio, she is exercising too little guidance control to qualify as responsible. The standards for reasons-responsivenss cannot be utterly idiosyncratic.

In order to be precise about who is responsible for their actions we need a position in between 'always responsive to reasons' (perfection) and almost never responsive to reasons (insanity). The account by Fischer and Ravissa is far too complex to repeat in detail here, but roughly they argue that to be reasons responsive a person must, in a wide variety of possible circumstances, exhibit an understandable pattern of recognizing reasons, be capable of acting on a subset of those reasons, and recognize some reasons as moral reasons.

These conditions are meant to exclude the insane and young children, thus exempting them from responsibility, but include people who maintain a grip on reality by recognizing reasons but who in many contexts fail to act on them because of a weak will or intentional wrongdoing. There are problems here, however. Reasons must exhibit an understandable pattern, but to whom must these reasons be understandable? It cannot be that the reasons have to be understandable only to the agent herself – the insane presumably understand their reasons though no one else can. We've already ruled out ideally objective standards for assessing reasons as too strong. Fischer and Ravissa must have in mind the sorts of reasons an average person might understand. However, this begins to resemble Strawson's approach in which judgements about responsibility depend on a conventional practice of holding people responsible.

Furthermore, assignments of responsibility do not always depend on the coherence of a pattern of reasoning. One of the stipulations that Fischer and Ravissa make for what counts as an understandable pattern is that if an agent would have recognized a sufficient reason for doing otherwise, then she must also recognize other similar reasons and assign appropriate weights to their relative importance. Imagine that Gordon breaks his promise to help his disabled mother move this weekend because he wanted to watch his favourite team play football. But suppose Gordon would have kept his promise if his mother had called and pleaded with him, and would have kept it if he had really liked the apartment she was moving into, but not if she and her belongings were to be thrown out on the street by the landlord if she doesn't vacate her present abode. Gordon's responsiveness to reasons is so haphazard that his thinking appears to lack any coherence. However, I doubt that we ought to conclude that he is not responsible. Intuitively, it would not be unfair to hold him responsible for breaking his promise. The condition that the pattern or reasoning must be understandable is too strong since we can imagine a case (Gordon) in which a person's reasoning pattern is not understandable yet we still hold him responsible.

Suppose that Christina, who has a dead-end job, falsely tells her new boyfriend she has received a lucrative promotion at her company in order to impress him. However, suppose that Christina would have told the truth had her favourite song about trust come on the radio, had she needed sympathy because her tennis game was falling apart, or if she wanted to prove people wrong who said he was only after her money, of which she has very little. Christina's reasoning is incoherent. But I think I know people who reason in this way and we rightly hold them responsible for their actions. So it doesn't look like having an understandable process of reasoning is necessary for moral responsibility.

Furthermore, it is not obvious we are ever in a position to know very much about the degree to which a person is responsive to reasons. To use one of Fischer and Ravissa's examples, imagine a pleasure seeker named Brown who spends most of his time in a stupor induced by a drug called Plezu, which is non-addictive but really fun. He recognizes that there are lots of reasons why he shouldn't take this drug first thing every morning, but it turns out that the only thing that will stop him is being told that injecting the drug one more time will kill him. He is responsive to this reason and this reason only. Brown is not the brightest of lights, but Fischer and Ravissa argue that he is nevertheless responsible because there is at least one reason he responds to – the threat of death. He is weakly reactive but nevertheless in control. His capacity for practical reason is functioning but defective.

However, the fact that Brown will respond to the incentive to avoid death is not an indicator that his obsession with Plezu is under control. Avoiding death is an incentive most persons will respond to regardless of their condition. Even addicts or people suffering from severe compulsions may respond to the threat of death, though they lack control when other incentives are offered. Is Brown deliberating about what to do and simply assigning inordinate weight to the pursuit of pleasure or has his obsession with pleasure suspended his capacity to deliberate until confronted with the threat of death?

Fischer and Ravissa argue that if an agent can react to one incentive then he can react to any incentive. But it is by no means obvious that practical reason works in this way. It might be the case that compulsions and obsessions can be narrowly focused to resist some incentives and not others and yet remain compulsions. If this is the case, reacting to a reason is not sufficient to qualify an agent as responsible. I'm not sure that we know enough about human psychology to distinguish between a mechanism that is functioning but defective and a mechanism that is not functioning. Intuitively there is a difference but in particular cases it will be hard to know.

However, once again intuitively it seems that Brown is responsible, not because he is, in fact, in control (since we do not know whether he is or not) but because we have the expectation that people should not succumb to pleasure to the extent Brown has. Pleasure, unlike addiction, is not the sort of thing that should so persistently overwhelm our cognitive capacities. We have the expectation that people should have that sort of control. Social interaction requires it. It is clear that some level of minimal rationality and the absence of debilitating pathologies is required for moral responsibility but specifying the precise conditions is no easy task.

The upshot of these objections to the account of guidance control is that Strawson's considerations best account for our attributions of responsibility. The lack of access to our motivational states means that for practical purposes we cannot rely solely on objective criteria for making judgements about control. In many contexts, we will not know enough about a particular person's control mechanism. Thus, our practice will be guided by pragmatic constraints regarding the kinds of judgements we must make to allow social life to flourish. It is not surprising that the reactive attitudes will be regulated by the perceived need to hold people responsible for certain kinds of behaviour, since to not do so would be disruptive, impractical, etc. Cognitive science may in the end discover much about our control mechanisms, but until we have this understanding in hand we will have to rely on judgements about how our practices of praise and blame help us sustain the norms required for social life.

These criticisms point out limitations in Fischer and Ravissa's account and highlight the fact that there is no escaping Strawson's general insight that assignments of responsibility are governed by the needs of social life. But the view I want to adopt is Strawson with a difference, because I think we need to reject Strawson's view that assignments of responsibility are not based on *any* independent reasons outside the framework of human social life. Recall that the problem with Strawson's view is that it leaves no room to criticize our social practices of assigning praise and blame. The value of Fischer and Ravissa's account is that it directs us to look at a relevant independent reason – the degree of control an agent has in the actual sequence of events that produces an action – that serves as a constraint on our practices of praise and blame. What we need, for this critical perspective on our practices, are standards that enable us to defend a claim that particular practices are unfair.

Awareness of guidance-control mechanisms helps us to set the normative bar for what level of reponsibility we insist on. In other words responsibility is not mitigated by bad luck or determinism. It is mitigated by lack of control but only when such mitigation does not violate normative requirements embedded in social life. Fischer and Ravissa's view is valuable because it puts pressure on those normative requirements. We have to weigh fairness to agents against the demands of social life and make mutual accommodation when possible, though, as I argued in Chapter 2, how we do this and when will not be a matter of principle but of contextual judgement. This judgement will be guided especially by how much we can plausibly discern about a person's motivations.

The fact that we suspect that guidance control breaks down when responsiveness to reasons or opportunities for self-reflection are limited puts pressure on our social practices and provides impetus to reform. Fischer and Ravissa have shown us that questions about guidance control are the right questions to ask, and criteria of guidance control can function independently of worries about determinism. But the needs of social life will inevitably intrude when criteria for control are short-circuited by the vagaries of human psychology.

REFERENCES AND SUGGESTIONS FOR FURTHER READING

Fischer, John and Ravissa, Mark (1998), *Responsibility and Control: A Theory of Moral Responsibility*, Cambridge: Cambridge University Press.

Kane, Robert (1996), *The Significance of Free Will*, New York: Oxford University Press.

Strawson, P. F. (1962), 'Freedom and Resentment', in *Proceedings of the British Academy*. Vol. 48.

EPILOGUE

We dwell in a valley of uncertainty and hope, bounded by our limitations and the relationships that enable us to manage these limitations and flourish despite them. There is no way to get back behind the limitations or the relationships to find something more fundamental that will anchor them. There is nothing we need to know about ethics that cannot be discovered in the smile in a child's voice, or the hesitation in a lover's caress. When we genuinely experience such things we know that no authority is required to certify them. But as Aristotle points out, we can fail to realize what is in our nature, so philosophy is a reminder. Ethics begins in the opening that freedom provides – the thought that things should be other than they are and the confidence to make that future concrete. But that opening is made possible by that smile and that hesitation, and the ability to laugh at the irony that ethics is perhaps the most vulnerable of human goods.

INDEX